How to Predict Elections

"Though this be madness, yet there is method in 't."

—SHAKESPEARE: *Hamlet,* ACT II, SCENE ii

LOUIS H. BEAN

How to Predict

Elections

Alfred A. Knopf

NEW YORK, 1948

Preface

Twelve years ago I fell "in love" at first sight with a half-page tabulation of election statistics, and I have been grateful to the *World Almanac* ever since. This half page contained nothing more than the percentages of the presidential vote received by the Democratic candidates in the elections from 1896 to 1932 in each of the forty-eight states; but that compact record showed so many systematic facts about the nation's political behavior and suggested so many fascinating possibilities for fruitful research that much of my spare time since then has been devoted to cultivating that vast field. Even with the primitive, easily understood tools that I have used, the field has yielded well.

My first effort to share my enthusiasm in the newly acquired hobby was a brochure entitled *Ballot Behavior*, published in 1940 by the American Council on Public Affairs. In the present book I have incorporated the results of further research and continued interest. The methods of analysis first set forth in 1940 I have used in connection with subsequent elections. Some of the findings constitute the main body of the present book. Several passages from *Ballot Behavior* have been used in presenting similar topics in this book.

The presentation and analysis of political facts in both *Ballot Behavior* and this volume are still, I believe, unique. In 1948 as in 1940 the findings and forecasts are offered to the public with the reserve inherent in presenting any new method of political-science investigation. Both the investigator and the reader must keep their minds open for modifications in approach and the possibility of other interpretations.

This book purposely avoids discussion of personalities and organized political effort as factors in elections. By dealing strictly

vii

in terms of facts and figures I of course fall into the same kind of error as do political leaders and bosses when they discuss politics and personalities without facts and figures.

Friends who want forecasts always to go right have questioned the wisdom of publishing studies in predicting elections in a year so strongly charged with political and economic uncertainties. They fear that 1948 might mark the beginning of postwar price deflation and business depression, and in addition, if the Wallace third party is at all effective in a few key states, analyses based largely on past experience might go wrong and "all bets would be off." I naturally appreciate and to some extent share their concern, but, after all, every election year has its great uncertainties. Furthermore, studies based on past experience are useful not only for anticipating results but also for judging the extent to which new situations cause results to depart from the expected.

I wish to acknowledge my indebtedness to Professor Harwood Childs of Princeton University and to Professor Paul Lazarsfeld of Columbia University, who for several years have urged me to make my studies in voting behavior generally available for use in classes in political science and public opinion.

My appreciation also goes to Mr. Allen Goldfine, who not only was interested in seeing my studies in published form, but sensed that his wish would be more readily fulfilled if some of the costs of spare-time research were not allowed to compete with the high cost of living.

I am indebted to Miss Mirriam Barrow for her patience and co-operation in preparing the charts on short notice, to Miss Catherine V. Shea for her keen interest in the subject matter and for many helpful suggestions, as well as for assistance in typing the manuscript, and to Miss Lillian Hornick for her valiant help in meeting a deadline.

There are two other persons to whom I am greatly indebted and to whom the readers of this book are indebted even more. Mr. Anthony Netboy rendered valuable editorial assistance and offered helpful criticism of passages that might have bogged the reader down in too many figures. Mrs. Dorothy Bean, after putting up with this hobby for some years, took a keen interest in saving the reader from unnecessary words and "gobbledegook."

Louis H. Bean

Table of Contents

CHAPTER 1: Politics in a Statistical Mirror 3
2: Political Tides, In and Out 12
3: The New Deal Tide 22
4: The President's "Coattail" 31
5: Ringing Doorbells 37
6: When Business Cycle Meets Political Cycle 50
7: The Power of Third Parties 62
8: Political Patterns 78
9: Issues That Divide 90
10: As Your State Goes, So Goes the Nation 105
11: Who Gets the Electoral Votes? 123
12: Predict If You Must 137
13: Why Polls Go Right and Wrong 148
14: 1948 and the Incoming Tide 161

STATISTICAL APPENDIX

TABLE 1: Numbers Voting as Per Cent of Total Population, Presidential Elections, 1888–1944 177
2: Number of Eligible Voters and Votes Cast in 1940 Presidential Election, by States 178
3: Popular Vote for President, 1888–1944 179
4: Percentage of Total Vote Cast for Third Parties in 1912 and 1924 Presidential Elections, by States 180
5: Presidential Elections, 1852–1944 (Per Cent of Popular Vote Cast for Democratic, Republican, and Other Candidates) 181
6: Democratic Percentage of Two-Party Presidential Vote, by States, 1896–1944 182
7: Democratic Percentage of Total Presidential Vote, by States, 1896–1944 184

TABLE 8: *State Democratic Percentages of Two-Party Presidential Vote Corresponding to National Democratic Percentages of 40 to 60*   186

9: *Vote for Members of House of Representatives, 1928–1946*   188

10: *Party Divisions of Senate and House of Representatives from 1855 (34th Congress) to 1947–9 (80th Congress)*   189

11: *Party Membership in House of Representatives, 1854–1946*   190

12: *Political Tides: Membership in Congress and Two-Party Vote for President, 1852–1946*   191

13: *Indexes of Voting Flexibility, 1896–1936 (by rank of States in 1896–1904 index)*   192

14: *Index of Business Activity, June and October 1854–1947 (per cent deviations from normal)*   193

15: *Illustration of Religion as a Factor in Presidential Elections: 1928, by States*   194

16: *Illustration of Nationality as a Factor in Presidential Elections: 1940, 1944, by States*   195

References   196

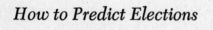

How to Predict Elections

Chapter 1:

Politics in a Statistical Mirror

Between the first part of this book, which analyzes the New Deal political tide, and the last chapter, which depicts the political tide of the future, the reader will find many of the hints, cues, and data useful in predicting elections. Political fluctuations are no more mysterious than business fluctuations. It is now quite common for variations in the nation's business and agriculture, in employment, production and prices, and wages and profits, to be portrayed and explained statistically. Much has been learned about the cycles of business and agriculture, but forecasting them is still an art rather than a science. In similar manner I have found that voting behavior, portrayed statistically, offers valuable keys to an explanation of the marked swings in American politics and helps to form a basis for judging political trends in the immediate future.

The New Deal political tide reached its peak in 1936 when Democrats obtained 62 per cent of the two-party vote for president and elected nearly 80 per cent of their candidates for

Congress. In 1946 the Democrats elected only 43 per cent of the 80th Congress. Republicans took this to be a mandate to undo much of what the New Deal stood for. Did that mark the end of the New Deal Democratic tide and the beginning of a prolonged period of Republican dominance? As the reader becomes familiar with some of the major reasons given in this book for changes in the Republican-Democratic balance, he will be able to answer this question more on the basis of facts and less on wish, guess, or intuition.

The two major parties that now control the political and economic destinies of the nation have alternately dominated the presidency and Congress for nearly a century. During that period American citizens have responded at the polls to liberal and conservative issues and personalities, to prosperity and depression, and to crises of war and peace. The past century has witnessed three major conflicts—one civil war and two world wars. We have had several business and agricultural depressions which affected all regions and population groups so profoundly that the party in power was thrown out of office, not to return until a later and similar depression occurred. We have had some unusually strong presidential candidates campaigning on major issues, such as Bryan's demand for the monetization of silver in 1896, which pitted the conservative, money-minded East against the mineral-minded West; or Al Smith's Catholic faith, which divided North and South, and his promise to repeal prohibition in 1928; or the threat of war that split the country in a more complex manner, East and West against the middle, in 1916 and 1940. There have also been elections in which the so-called *liberal* citizens of the metropolitan areas, Boston, New York, and Chicago, voted predominantly Democratic while their rural cousins in up-state New York or down-state Illinois supported the Republicans as usual. Most of these cleavages are reflected in the statistical mirror of national and regional voting behavior for the period 1928–46, which embraces the New Deal tide.

Every presidential and congressional campaign offers the analyst an opportunity to isolate particular elements that promise to dominate the election and to correlate them with the political factors always present. In this series of studies I have used the familiar adage: "As Maine goes, so goes the nation," for predicting the 1936 election; business factors in forecasting the 1938 congressional campaigns; the trend in the New Deal tide and prewar isolationist sentiment in determining the outcome of the 1940 presidential race; and a combination of past trends, size of the expected vote, and economic conditions in assaying Democratic chances in the 1946 congressional elections. Each of these factors, supplemented by an examination of third-party impact on voting behavior, has a bearing on what happens in 1948 and later elections.

To develop statistical proof for the adage "As Maine goes, so goes the nation," was a fruitful venture. According to the popular historical interpretation of this adage, the party that wins in the September election of state officers in Maine triumphs in the national elections in November. In September 1932 Maine elected the Republican slate of state and local officers, but the national result in November was a Democratic landslide. The adage seemed thoroughly discredited. An examination of the record, however, restored my faith in the old saying; fundamentally it still spoke truth. The Democratic (or Republican) percentage of the total vote cast in Maine fluctuated in accordance with the variation of the Democratic (or Republican) percentage of the total national vote. On the basis of this parallelism, I predicted in September 1936, when Maine went 45 per cent Democratic, that the nation would give Roosevelt about 60 per cent of the popular vote. He actually received 62 per cent.

With the voting record for every state reduced to a simple formula—the Democratic or Republican percentage of the total ballots cast in a number of elections—further examination revealed that not only Maine but many other states are barometers of national voting behavior. Despite the many influences that shape the course of elections in the forty-eight states, there emerges a fairly systematic pattern for the nation. Any oscillation in the national pendulum has reverberations in each state and even in many counties. The behavior of one state in a given election can consequently be translated into the corresponding behavior of the nation as a whole, which can in turn be translated into the corresponding behavior of each of the other forty-seven states. This principle, which I first used in 1936, enabled me to predict that if the nation went 60 per cent Democratic, as foreshadowed by the Maine election and other local indications, the Democratic Party would carry all but three states: Maine, Vermont, and Pennsylvania. It actually carried all but two: Maine and Vermont.

This systematic pattern of political behavior (elaborated in subsequent chapters) has been generally overlooked. It is an important tool, however, in political research and analysis as well as in forecasting the 1948 and subsequent presidential elections.

It may be likened to the relationships that exist in our commodity markets. Ordinarily, fluctuations in the price of wheat at, say, Chicago, are accompanied by similar fluctuations in all other central or local markets where dealers, millers, exporters, feeders, farmers, and speculators deal in the commodity, because the essential facts with regard to supply and demand are known everywhere. Prices at local shipping points in rural Kansas, for example, differ from those at Kansas City and Chicago only by the amount of freight and other minor costs. Consequently, if wheat at a Kansas shipping point rises ten cents per bushel, it is reasonable to assume on the basis of long experience that there has been a comparable change at other shipping points and central markets, unless some unusual local factor of supply or demand is responsible.

The existence of an extraordinarily uniform voting pattern in many states and counties must be due to the fact that there are similar economic and social groups in each state and locality. Some communities may have more laborers than others, some more farmers, professional people, or businessmen. This economic composition of the population tends to determine whether a community is predominantly Republican or predominantly Democratic. In every state and county there are people who respond alike to certain nation-wide economic and social issues. The mere fact that a county or state has never given the Democrats more than 40 nor less than 10 per cent of its vote does not mean that its political behavior is not useful for analytical or forecasting purposes. The important point is that fluctuations between 10 and 40 per cent in that community correspond to fluctuations in the same direction—but not quantity—in many states, counties, and the country as a whole. In fact, a 10 per cent loss or gain by the Democrats throughout the nation may result in a corresponding shift of more or less than 10 per cent in many communities, depending on their political *flexibility*.

In judging the outcome of a presidential election, knowledge of the party line-up by states is an absolute necessity, since candidates must obtain a majority of electoral votes. A majority of the popular vote alone is not sufficient for election. Therefore the systematic relationships, which can be reduced to arithmetical terms, between the way the nation and each state vote are extremely useful and for that reason will be presented in this book in some detail.

The political horizon in 1938 was dominated by the setback to the New Deal recovery programs. Industrial production fell sharply during the last half of 1937 and first quarter of 1938, and unemployment, which had been diminishing since 1933, again increased. This unexpected recession boded ill for the Democratic candidates in the congressional elections in November. An examination of the effect of similar business recessions on elections in the previous eighty years, and on shifts in the position of the major party in the lower house, showed us that the Democrats were bound to lose many seats. I predicted in March 1938 that their membership in the lower house would decline from 79 per cent in 1936 to between 60 and 65 per cent. In the elections eight months later the Democrats retained only 61 per cent of the seats. It was not until 1946—and this may surprise many readers—that a decline in industrial activity and curtailment of consumer purchasing power again appeared as a factor in determining election results. Will a business depression again appear in the foreground of the political scene in 1948, 1950, 1952, or later?

In 1940 the outcome of the presidential election seemed to hinge on whether the so-called Republican tide, beginning with the Republican gains in 1938, was rising or ebbing, and whether the third-term bogy and isolationism would fatally reduce Roosevelt's chances. The issue of isolationism versus internationalism, in so far as it could be studied historically in the analogous election of 1916, pointed to losses in Democratic strength in the Midwest and Northwest, with offsetting gains in the East and Far West. The net effect of the third-term issue could not be adequately appraised except through current polls of public opinion, and these indicated that the Democrats would not lose many votes on this score. Assuming that the course of the New Deal tide might be the dominant factor in the 1940 election, I examined the characteristics of the several political tides since

1854 and the reasons for their upturns and downturns. This analysis led to the conclusion that if no major business depression set in before the fall of 1940 and no nation-wide third party entered the race, the country as a whole would give 54–55 per cent to the Democrats, compared with 62 per cent in 1936. Roosevelt was elected with 55 per cent of the two-party vote.

The 1944 election offered an opportunity to study the factor of turnout and its influence on the Democratic-Republican balance, a factor that is ordinarily more important in off-year congressional than in presidential elections. The Republican victories in the congressional election of 1942, and the several by-elections in 1943 to fill vacancies, made political analysts sensitive to the size of the vote. While these gains were hailed as a continuation of the Republican tide that had set in after 1936 and as foreshadowing a Republican victory in 1944, an examination of the 1942–3 Republican gains showed clearly that they were largely the result of voting apathy. Few citizens took congressional elections seriously when the country was engaged in war. It was found that, as a rule, the smaller the total vote cast, the smaller the Democratic proportion. On the strength of this fact, it was possible to predict early in 1944 that the Democratic candidate would receive about 53 per cent of the popular vote. Roosevelt actually won 53.8 per cent. What does this method of forecasting a presidential election reveal for 1948 and after?

The 1946 election offered an opportunity to examine in greater detail the behavior of voters in mid-term congressional elections, and to develop a unique method of measuring the effect of such elections on the number of seats each party is likely to control. It is fairly common knowledge that many Congressmen have been elected by virtue of running on the ticket of a winning presidential candidate. This analysis was important in 1946. It clearly indicated that if the Democrats failed to bring many apathetic citizens to the polls, their margin in the House would be wiped out and their membership reduced from 56 per cent in the 79th Congress to only 45 per cent in the 80th. Actually, they elected only 43 per cent of their candidates. An understanding of the forces that shaped the 1946 elections made it possible to point out, even before the opinion polls of 1947 were taken, that the Republican victories in 1946 were in part ephemeral and did

not necessarily mark the beginning of Republican domination of
Congress for a prolonged period.

It has been observed that, in the ninety years from 1856 to
1946, the party that gained control of Congress in a mid-term
congressional election usually placed its presidential candidate
in the White House two years later. When in 1946 the Republicans captured the Congress, many people expected them to win
the presidency in 1948. My analysis indicates that this mid-term
formula should not be accepted blindly. Indeed, there is no guarantee that the elections in 1948 and after might not give us the
reverse of 1946, a Republican president and a Democratic Congress.

Most of the factors which have been dominant in elections
from 1928 to 1946 will influence the 1948 and succeeding campaigns. For this reason they are treated separately in this book;
first historically, and later in relation to the 1946 and future
elections.

In spite of the fact that several statistical analyses which have
proved useful in appraising and anticipating the results of presidential and congressional elections are presented here, the reader
is warned against expecting this book to give him a precise and
fixed method of predicting elections. The main objective has
been to present basic facts so organized that they may serve as
a foundation or springboard for the application of one's judgment.

As in the field of economics, it is necessary to distinguish between the art of describing relationships that have held good
in the past and the art of forecasting. Forecasting as often prac-
ticed is nothing more than the assumption that trends observable
in the past, and relationships based on past experience, will hold
in the immediate future. The real art of forecasting, however,
involves an accurate appraisal of whether new factors may or
may not appear to alter the observable trends and past relationships.

Anyone who has an elementary knowledge of arithmetic will
be able to move comfortably through the following chapters.
Political tides over a period of years are here represented simply
by the changing percentage of the presidential vote cast in the
various elections by the Democratic Party, or the proportion of
the House or Senate seats won by either party. The effects of

business conditions, various political issues, and size of the vote are all measured in the same statistical terms. There is, of course, no particular reason for expressing these political facts in terms of Democratic rather than Republican percentages, except that these studies have been made during a period of Democratic dominance. Any Democratic percentage of a two-party vote, say 45 per cent, can be converted readily—merely by subtracting it from 100—into the Republican figure, 55 per cent.

Forecasting elections during the course of a campaign, or even before the campaign is under way, may at first glance appear to have no practical utility. Actually, knowledge of what is likely to occur, and the magnitude of the forces that will bring it about, may be of considerable practical use in politics as in economics. Politicians and campaign managers interested in shaping election results can more readily plan their strategy if they know whether their candidate leads with a narrow or a wide margin. Organizations can more effectively conduct a doorbell-ringing campaign, and candidates more intelligently choose when and how to run, if they know whether time, tide, business conditions, and political issues are in their favor and, especially, by how much.

It is hoped that even a cursory perusal of the material presented here will enlarge somewhat the average voter's knowledge of political fluctuations and give new interest to presidential campaigns and elections.

To accomplish this aim, the next chapter will acquaint the reader with the general course of the Republican-Democratic tides so that he may see where the two-party balance stood as of November 1946, and where it stands on the eve of the 1948 presidential race. This will be followed by an examination of the rise and decline of the New Deal tide in the light of political and economic forces.

I shall measure the pulling power of the president's coattail, the influence of voter interest or apathy as reflected in the turnout at the polls, and the effect of business and agricultural conditions. I shall gauge the extent to which religious preferences sway normal voting habits. Then we shall conduct a statistical tour to selected parts of the country to observe how nationality or cultural groups respond to the issue of internationalism versus isolationism. I shall note how and where third parties affect the fortunes of the two major parties. Then I shall examine the presidential voting record in the forty-eight states to see which follow a common pattern and which depart from the general trend, and why. On the basis of these findings I shall show which states go as the nation goes, and then draw up a master tabulation to indicate at a glance, first, which states would fall into the Republican and Democratic columns if the nation voted 46, 48, 50, 52, 54, or 56 per cent Democratic; and, second, how many electoral votes each party could expect in each contingency.

I shall take a look at election polls, since the sampling of public opinion is now a generally accepted feature of political analysis and judgment and serves to bring historical trends up to date. I shall note how well they foreshadow later election results. Polling is essentially the art of obtaining from a remarkably small sample an indication as to how the entire population of the country, state, or community reacts to a particular issue or candidate. To illustrate the problem of getting a good cross-section of public opinion, I shall describe how I organized a hypothetical corporation in 1940 with Roosevelt, Wallace, Willkie, McNary, Hoover, and Garner—all expert poll-takers in their home counties —as the regional field staff and board of directors; and then, on the strength of the success of this parent corporation in predicting the 1940 election, how we created two equally successful hypothetical subsidiaries.

Finally we shall synthesize the several political elements studied in this book and launch the reader on his own venture in forecasting the results of the 1948 and subsequent elections. For this purpose we shall supply him with a guide (not a forecast) in the form of a typical tide from 1936 to 1956, with which his own forecasts may be compared. If there are readers who, like me, enjoy prospecting for gold among systematic facts as well as theoretical speculation, they will find appended to this book suggestive materials for such prospecting.

Chapter 2:

Political Tides, In and Out

Political tides are like the unsubstantiated sea serpent that appears periodically along the Atlantic coast. They are discussed in every presidential election year by popular political analysts and commentators, but without much factual demonstration.

Just as the length, size, and shape of the sea monster vary with the person recounting the tale, so the duration and dimensions of political tides and the extent to which they are influenced by business conditions, third parties, war, or other issues vary according to the student, analyst, or commentator. Depending on the analyst, the tides are said to last eight, twelve, or even twenty years.

From time to time studies of political tides appear in scholarly journals. In the 1940 Winter issue of the *Yale Review* Professor Arthur M. Schlesinger, Sr., of Harvard, examines the duration of liberal and conservative movements in American politics. He seeks to prove that periods of liberalism, when new Federal legislation is concerned chiefly with human issues, alternate with periods of conservatism when new legislation is devoted mainly to property rights. These periods, he finds, differ in duration but tend to last from fifteen to eighteen years. In 1940, according to Schlesinger, we were in the midst of a liberal tide that originated in 1931, due to last until 1947 or 1948 and to be followed by a period of conservatism that would terminate in 1963. The loss of control of Congress by the Democrats in 1946 appears to be a fair corroboration of his conclusion, but my analyses point to another interpretation of what the future political tide could be.

What is a political tide? Where should we go to find it? Should we look for it in the changing number of votes cast for president, senators, or congressmen, or in the seats each party controls in the House and Senate? Having found it, how can we measure it? What does a tide look like? How often does it come in and how often go out? How regular is its course, and how large are the waves it creates?

There is no quantitive measure of the American political tide beyond the general fact that for a period of nearly one hundred years Republican administrations of the Federal government have several times been displaced by Democratic administrations.

As a matter of fact, our notion of what constitutes a Republican or a Democratic administration is not too precise. Did we have a Democratic administration after the 1918 election when Democratic President Woodrow Wilson, in spite of his specific appeal, was given a predominantly Republican Congress with which to thresh out the League of Nations issue in 1919–20? Did we have a Republican administration in the 1929–32 depression period when Republican President Herbert Hoover had a Congress divided about evenly between Democrats and Republicans? Did we have a Democratic administration in 1946–8 when a predominantly Republican Congress and a Democratic President struggled—often at cross-purposes—with the enormous task of checking postwar inflation, sharing our goods with a destitute and starving Europe, and helping the United Nations establish a stable basis for world peace?

How, then, are we to chart the political tide? Should it be a measure of the vote for president for the past hundred years or more? Or should it be based on the vote for members of the Senate or House?

We can exclude for the present the record of voting for the

Senate—the least satisfactory of the three possibilities—for the simple reason that we didn't begin to elect senators by popular vote until 1916. Moreover, only a third of the ninety-six senators are elected every two years. The record of voting in presidential elections is probably a better measure of political tides than the senatorial vote since it goes as far back as 1824, when electors began to be chosen by popular vote rather than by state legislators. But the record of voting in congressional elections should be even better for our purposes, since all the members of the lower house are elected every two years. Furthermore, this record offers a statistical measure of our shift to and from Republican and Democratic extremes back to 1854, when the present Republican Party was born. For these reasons we shall study political tides first in the changing membership of the two major parties in the lower house.

Division of the 435 seats in Congress has varied greatly since World War I. At the opening of the 67th Congress, elected in 1920, the Republicans had 300 seats to 132 for the Democrats, or 82 more than the minimum of 218 required for control of the House. By the time the 73rd Congress took office, in 1933, the pendulum had swung to the other side. The lower house elected in 1936 consisted of 333 Democrats, 89 Republicans, and 13 from other parties. This gave the Democrats 79 per cent of the two-party total, the Republicans only 21 per cent. The political tide in Congress in the course of sixteen years thus may be said to have shifted from a position 31 per cent Democratic in 1920 to 79 per cent in 1936 (or from a Republican peak of 69 per cent to a Democratic peak of 79). As we compute similar percentages for every congressional election back to 1854, we see that only a few times has the political tide swung so widely as between 1920 and 1936.

The complete record of the Democratic proportion of members of the House of Representatives since 1854 is contained in chart 1. In 1854 the Democrats had 44 per cent of the two-party membership, the Republicans 56 per cent. Two years later the Democrats regained control of the lower house by winning 59 per cent of the seats. Since then there have been three prolonged periods of Republican domination. The first was the fourteen-year period from 1858 to 1872; the second, the fourteen-year period from 1894 to 1908; and the third, the twelve years after World War I.

DEMOCRATIC TIDES AND UPWARD TREND

CHART 1

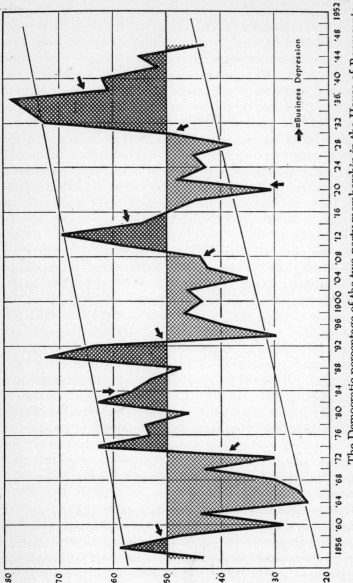

Democratic Percentage

The Democratic percentage of the two-party membership in the House of Representatives, 1854–1946, has fluctuated widely above and below 50 per cent. The alternating periods of Democratic and Republican control were associated with major depressions. Over the entire period there appears to have been an upward trend in Democratic strength. (1860–8 not strictly comparable, since Southern states are not represented. See also charts 2 and 3.)

↓ =Business Depression

The Democrats have also enjoyed three periods of dominance in Congress since 1860. The first embraced fourteen of the eighteen years between 1874 and 1892. The second was a brief six-year interlude between 1910 and 1918. And the third, which most of us watching the election of 1948 and anticipating those of the 1950's know best, ran for sixteen years from 1930 to 1946.

The alternating sequence of Republican and Democratic control since 1854 raises the very important question whether the Republicans, having gained a majority in both House and Senate in 1946, entered upon another prolonged period of domination due to last ten to sixteen years as in the past. The answer to this question, as to lesser political mysteries, must be reserved for the last chapter, since a good deal of material must be analyzed before we can say yes or no.

There are one or two aspects of the Republican and Democratic tides that are worth observing immediately. First, we may note that in three instances the Republicans gained control of the House only to lose it in the next election. They had control in 1854, but lost it in 1856, then regained it in 1858. They won ascendancy in 1880, but lost in the next three elections; recovered in 1888, but fell back in 1890 and 1892. Does the Republican victory in 1946 suggest another of these brief episodes or the beginning of a longer stay in power, as in 1858, 1894, and 1918, when that party came in and dominated Congress for six or seven elections?

Another striking feature of political tides is that they appear to be *moving* along a rising Democratic trend. You will see this more clearly if you will take a piece of string or an elastic band and stretch it across chart 1 so that it passes through the high points, 1856 and 1912. The trend line will reveal that there has been a tendency for Democratic peaks to touch higher and higher levels, with 1890 and 1936 somewhat above the trend. If you will now stretch the string or elastic band so that it passes through the low points of the Democratic tides—1864 and 1928—you will find that these points have also tended to move upward. Only the low point of 1920 fell somewhat below the trend. Interestingly enough, the 1946 election results were not far out of line with the Democratic percentage indicated by this rising trend. Shall we therefore conclude that from now on the Democrats normally will control about 60 per cent of the House, varying between 45 and 75 per cent, whereas in the 1860's and 1870's they normally elected about 45 per cent of the House members, varying between 30 and 60 per cent?

An investigation of the reasons for this long-time rise in Democratic strength in Congress and the prospect of its continuing in that direction would be worth while. My surmise is that the rise is related to the fact that more and more of the population have become concentrated in the larger industrial cities where the bulk of the Democratic vote is to be found. In 1860 only 20 per cent of the total population was urban; by 1940 the proportion had risen to 56.5 per cent. Over these decades the Republican Party, which at its inception embraced labor groups, gained the reputation of being dominated by big-business interests. In the 1850's and 1860's the Republicans had the support of the bulk of labor and progressive elements. At the turn of the century labor leaders found themselves less welcome in the councils of the Republican Party, and in the 1930's and 1940's the labor and progressive groups had switched much of their support to the Democratic Party.

Like the tides in nature, political tides are the result of many complex factors. But the abrupt shifts that brought about the six periods of alternating Republican and Democratic control of Congress are traceable to one major cause—business depressions. This does not mean that other factors have not played their part, but the record certainly indicates that the business factor has been consistently dominant.

The Democrats lost control in 1858—a year of depression. They regained it in 1874, after the great financial and industrial crash of 1873. The Republicans took over in 1894, after the financial and industrial collapse of 1893. The Democrats returned to power after the depression of 1908, but their strength began to wane with the depression of 1914 and they were definitely voted out with the depression of 1920. Democratic opportunity knocked again when the great boom of the 1920's collapsed and ushered in the vast unemployment of the early 1930's. The Democrats regained control of Congress in 1930, but began to toboggan with the recession of 1938. Were it not for these eight major industrial crises of the last century, the political tides would not have swung so widely. When booms turn to busts and full employment to unemployment and misery, the party in power—be it Democratic or

Republican—is usually turned out. Greater economic stability in the future would mean greater political stability.

If we want a *smoother* political tide than the sharp changes in the record of the lower house provide, we can find it in the party membership of the upper house. The greater regularity here rests on the fact that only one third of the senators stand for election every two years. Strictly speaking, this record is therefore not comparable with that of the lower house as a measure of changes in political sentiment. It is of course fully as important as the House record in measuring party strength. The legislation that emerges from our Federal law-making machine depends on the margin of votes each party controls in both the lower house and the Senate.

From 1854 to 1946, as shown in chart 2, the Senate was predominantly Republican except for 1878–80, 1892–4, 1912–18, and 1930–46, when the Democrats outnumbered their rivals. The election of 1930, the first after the financial crash of 1929, gave the Democrats an additional 8 seats, a total of 47. The election of 1932, at the depth of the depression, resulted in a further increase of 12, and by 1936 the Democratic total had risen to 75. With a meager 17 seats for Republicans and 4 for other parties, the Democrats had more than 80 per cent of the two-party total— the largest Democratic majority in the history of the Senate, and about as high as the Republican record majority of 1868.

The Republicans recaptured the Senate as well as lower house in 1946. But it took five elections, or ten years, for the Republican Party to wipe out the gains made by the Democrats in the preceding four elections (1928–36).

The political tide in the Senate as in the House has been moving on a rising Democratic trend. In the 1860's the Democrats controlled only about 20 per cent of the two-party seats; at the turn of the century, about 35 per cent; and in 1928, 42 per cent. It is not entirely a matter of hindsight to point out that the results of the 1946 election, restoring control of the Senate to the Republicans, were foreshadowed by this statistical record. The record said in effect that if the Democratic tide in the Senate which began to recede in 1938 continued to ebb, the party strength would fall below 50 per cent by 1946. This is exactly what happened.

Will the Republicans continue to gain in the next few years,

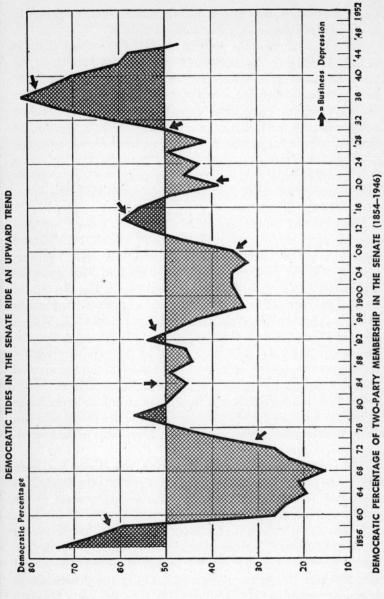

DEMOCRATIC TIDES IN THE SENATE RIDE AN UPWARD TREND

DEMOCRATIC PERCENTAGE OF TWO-PARTY MEMBERSHIP IN THE SENATE (1854-1946)

The year 1946 marked the end of a period of Democratic control similar to the period of Republican control ending in 1878. This record fluctuates less than the record in chart 1 because only one third of the Senate is elected every two years.

➡ = Business Depression

CHART 2

or will the Senate remain almost evenly divided for some time? Republican gains in 1948 were limited since only three senators outside the South were up for re-election. Is it likely that the tide will turn and that the Democrats will regain dominance during the next few years? Not as an answer to these questions but merely as a statistical fact, the reader may want to note again the low phase of the Democratic tide in the Senate for 1946–8 in relation to the rising trend of previous low points. If 1946–8 should mark the low point in the Democratic tide in the Senate, it would be statistically reasonable to anticipate (on the basis of the rising trend) that at the next peak, whenever it occurs, the Democrats would have 60 or 70 per cent of the total Senate membership.

The political tide in the two-party vote for president differs from the tide as seen in the membership of the House (chart 3) because presidential elections come every four years. While this tends to make for smoother, less erratic swings of the pendulum, it obscures a great deal of significant political history.

There is an underlying similarity in the pattern of the popular vote for president and party composition in Congress, especially if we recognize that congressional tides fluctuate about twice as widely as the party vote for president. On the average, a 5 per cent shift in the Democratic vote for president is accompanied by a 10 per cent shift in the Democratic proportion of membership in the House. This relationship is shown in chart 3.

In the eleven presidential elections since 1900 the correspondence between the two political tides, as the chart shows, has been quite close. The outstanding exception occurred in 1924, when LaFollette's third party competed, primarily, for Democratic votes. The two records are so closely interrelated that if we could forecast the one we would automatically be predicting the other.

Of chief interest to all of us is the political tide of 1928–46. What direction will it take? Since we are measuring it here in terms of Democratic percentages, we may call it the New Deal tide. A close-up of that tide, as well as the factors producing its rise and fall, will provide the historical basis for projecting the next phase in the Republican-Democratic struggle.

THE VOTE FOR PRESIDENT DETERMINES HIS CONGRESS, 1852–1946

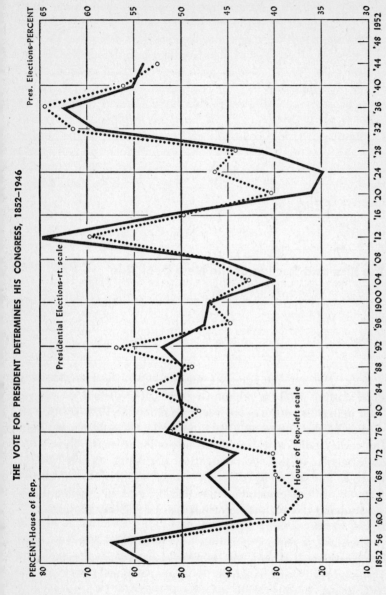

Democratic percentage of two-party vote for president and of two-party membership in House of Representatives. Note the general similarity between and the occasional discrepancies (1924, 1912, 1892). The congressional percentage fluctuates about twice as much as the presidential.

CHART 3

Chapter 3:

The Rise and Decline of the New Deal Tide

An understanding of the immediate past is always a good starting point for preliminary speculations about the future. That in itself is reason enough for examining the 1928–46 rise and decline of the Democratic Party in Congress more closely than the earlier political tides. There are other reasons. This is the most regular of the several political developments recorded in chart 1, and so many different events occurred to affect the fortunes of the Democratic Party that it forms an excellent basis for studying the anatomy of a political tide. Every move can be traced to one or more specific factors.

There are, of course, numerous ways of explaining and portraying elections. It would not be surprising to find as many as a thousand realistic explanations for any one national election. Why a thousand? Because there must be at least one Democratic and one Republican explanation for each of the 435 congressional and 32 senatorial contests. In order to discover the few outstanding facts of national importance that produced the latest political tide, we shall take an over-all approach and need not lose ourselves in the details of local political campaigns.

It will be sufficient to give a brief recital of the several dramatic developments that accompanied the rise of the Democratic Party to the highest peak of power in its history and its steep but jagged descent in the House and Senate. As the nation moved in the early 1930's from a business recession into deep depression, voters behaved as on former similar occasions; many of them deserted the party in power—the Republicans—for the opposite side. On the other hand, when the recovery of 1936-7 was succeeded by a sharp recession in 1937-8, many voters again changed their allegiance, this time from the Democratic to the Republican Party. Democratic strength continued to wane for the following ten years under the impact of such issues as third and fourth terms for Franklin D. Roosevelt, management-labor difficulties, war, wartime political apathy, and finally rationing and shortages of goods and materials in 1946. Many groups, driven by the force of the 1932 depression and 1933-6 recovery measures into the Democratic Party, dropped away.

The configuration and history of the New Deal political tide is sketched in chart 4. This chart shows ten stages in the rise and decline of the New Deal tide from 1928 to 1946. For each, numbered in sequence, a few admittedly incomplete topical reminders of the times are given. In 1928 as we were about to wind up the New Era in prosperity and mad speculation, Hoover received the largest vote on record up to that time, and the Republicans gained control of the House, leaving the Democrats with only 38 per cent of the seats. Confident of continued prosperity, the nation headed for the greatest speculative boom in our history. Its appalling collapse within a year of the Republican landslide marks the real beginning of the New Deal tide.

By the time the 1930 congressional elections took place, the agricultural and industrial depression was in full swing and the Democrats made their initial gain toward ultimate control of Congress. As a result of that first year of depression the Democrats gained 51 seats in the House—jumping from 163 to 214— only 4 short of a bare majority. The death of several Republican Congressmen between the election in November and the opening of Congress in March 1931 gave the Democrats the few marginal seats necessary to take control and organize the House.

As industry and agriculture went deeper into depression, with unemployment, business failures, and losses in farm income mounting to unheard-of proportions, the movement of voters to the Democratic side was accelerated. This shift was, surprisingly, greater in the traditionally Republican rural areas than in many industrial cities. By 1932 the tide attained record proportions; the Democrats not only captured the presidency but gained 99 Congressmen and 11 Senators. They now controlled 74 per cent of the seats in the lower house and 62 per cent in the Senate.

It is not far-fetched to attribute this reversal in the political balance almost entirely to the great business depression. The congressional elections of 1924, 1926, and 1928 had given no evidence of any upsurge in Democratic strength. On the other hand, the sudden rise after 1928 was strikingly paralleled by the jump in unemployment. Indeed, the parallel was so close that one is tempted to work out a simple formula for the relation between the two. Unemployment—about 3 per cent of the total labor force in 1929—increased to 9 per cent in 1930 and to 25 per cent in 1932. This 6-point rise in the year 1929–30 resulted in a 10-point increase in Democratic strength (as measured by the number of seats in the lower house). In 1932, with additional unemployment of 16 per cent of the labor force, the Democrats gained 26 points. While this trend is not the basis for determining an exact formula, it is nevertheless worth observing that as the depression became graver, the Democrats gained 16 per cent of the total seats in the House for every 10 per cent rise in unemployment of the nation's labor force. Another, and perhaps better, way of putting it is that with every increase of a million in unemployment the Republicans lost 14 seats in Congress.

New Deal legislation helped to swell the Democratic tide. The dominant influence came from the nation-wide interest in and support of the social and economic programs that were intended to reduce unemployment and lift industrial production as well as farm prices and farm income. The Democrats gained 9 seats in the 1934 election in spite of the general expectation that the party in power would lose ground as in former mid-term elections. We shall see in the next chapter that this gave clear evidence that the effect of the depression on the momentum of the Democratic tide had not yet spent itself.

In 1936 the Democrats reached the peak of their congressional

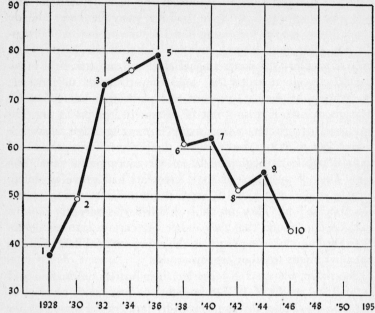

TEN STAGES IN THE NEW DEAL TIDE

Democratic Percentage

DEMOCRATIC PERCENTAGES OF THE TWO-PARTY MEMBERSHIP IN THE HOUSE OF REPRESENTATIVES, 1928–46

1) 1928, prosperity rising toward peak of speculative "boom and bust" in 1929.

2) 1930, sharp depression in agriculture and industry, small vote.

3) 1932, deep depression, 12 million unemployed; large, but normal, vote.

4) 1934, New Deal programs for relief and recovery under way. Unemployment reduced; drought and further rise in farm prices; small turnout.

5) 1936, New Deal programs for relief and recovery; higher living costs; concern over unbalanced Federal budget; largest vote on record.

6) 1938, sharp recession in industry and agriculture, labor-management difficulties; increase in unemployment; drive to pack Supreme Court; light vote.

7) 1940, third-term issue; continued unemployment; war in Europe, isolationist sentiment; largest vote on record.

8) 1942, war activity, unusually small turnout.

9) 1944, fourth-term issue; accumulating wartime dissatisfactions; small vote; millions in services abroad; wartime rationing; price control.

10) 1946, unusually small vote; removal of price control; rising living costs; material shortages; confusion in reconversion and foreign policy.

CHART 4

strength, the accumulated results of the New Deal relief and recovery programs. Yet, as we shall see later, there was already real evidence of the beginning of a Democratic decline, particularly in many agricultural counties and districts. In the Corn Belt states the 1934 congressional elections and the 1936 presidential election revealed that 1932 converts to the Democratic Party were beginning to return to their traditional affiliations. The great distress arising out of extremely low prices and the industrial depression caused many farmers to leave their firm Republican moorings, but with the sharp rise in farm prices, and with Republicans beginning to accept and promise much the same kind of programs as the Democrats had provided, many farmers apparently found it more comfortable to return to the Republican fold. They probably justified this seeming ingratitude on the ground that they didn't like certain features of the New Deal agricultural programs, the rising national debt, and the so-called favors to labor organizations.

The sharp, unexpected recession in industrial production and agricultural prices of 1937–8 brought the first major reversal in the New Deal tide. Prices received by farmers fell about 30 per cent between April 1937 and August 1938. Industrial production declined about as much during this four-month interval as during the sharp postwar depression of 1920–1, while unemployment, which had fallen during the recovery period to 5 millions, rose to nearly 9 millions. The drift from Democratic ranks in 1934 and 1936 was essentially local, concentrated in the rural areas, and did not then generally attract attention. The loss of Democratic congressional seats in the 1938 election was much more widespread and sensational.

Other factors besides the industrial recession, increased unemployment, and the fall in agricultural prices contributed to the 1938 political reversal. Chart 7 indicates that a small turnout of voters, characteristic of practically all mid-term elections, was a major factor. President Roosevelt's proposal and effort to pack the Supreme Court with six additional younger members to offset the conservatism of the "nine old men" alienated many voters. We have no way of judging what role this issue played in the 1938 election. However, we may be certain that the economic reversal, because of its magnitude, played its usual important part. In fact, a year before the 1938 election I considered the business situation so important as a political determinant that, on the strength of it alone, I predicted a decline in the Democratic percentage of seats in the House from 79 to 60–5. It actually fell to 61 per cent.

Two new factors show up in chart 4 to explain the 1940 election results: the anti-third-term feeling and isolationist sentiment. Europe was already completely involved in war and at the time of the 1940 election, as in 1916, we as a nation were not eager to enter it. Sentiment against participation was strongest in the Middle West, while interest in the war was keener in the Eastern and Far Western states—a repetition of the regional response in 1916. The third-term issue, combined with isolationism, undoubtedly kept the Democrats from recovering part of their 1938 losses in the 1940 general election. The third-term issue alone, it will be shown later, cost President Roosevelt about 1.5 million votes. It is true that business activity had improved and unemployment had been reduced in the previous two years, but the other issues —including our policy of aid to England, the mounting Federal debt, and dissatisfaction with labor laws—favored the Republicans more. Because of such factors the Democrats regained only 7 seats in the House instead of the 30 they would normally have added, given a combination of prosperity and a presidential election. This gave 62 per cent of the two-party membership to the Democrats and left the two parties in about the same relative position as in 1938.

The New Deal tide had now completed about half its downward swing from 1936 to 1946. The rest of the descent is marked by two additional substantial setbacks, those of 1942 and 1946. The Democrats nearly lost control of the House in 1942, chiefly because of a phenomenally small turnout. It is estimated in a subsequent chapter that fully 22 million voters who normally would have gone to the polls in a mid-term congressional election failed to vote in 1942. The chief reason for this indifference was that most citizens were preoccupied with the war effort, working long hours at good pay; there were no great issues in the congressional elections; and many persons had migrated to war centers and, even if they had wanted to vote, were too far away from their home districts. The unusual lack of voting interest played into the hands of the Republicans, for more potential Democratic voters stayed home than Republicans.

The majority of those who did vote followed traditional party lines. It was estimated by the Office of Public Opinion Research at Princeton that 86 per cent of those who claimed to be Republicans voted Republican in 1942, and of those who said they were Democrats, 81 per cent voted Democratic. Independents divided their ballots; 57 per cent voted Republican and 43 per cent Democratic. I estimate that of the shortage of 22 million votes about 13 million were Democratic and 9 million Republican. The Democrats lost 46 seats in the House and their total fell to 222. Had their losses extended to 5 more seats, they would have lost control completely. As it was, their margin was so narrow that the President's legislative programs were frequently caught in a stalemate.

As a result of the 1942 elections the Republicans optimistically believed that they would take over the presidency as well as Congress in 1944, and were encouraged in that hope by a number of local elections in 1943 and early 1944. As a matter of fact, the Republicans had gained much less ground between 1938 and 1942 than their optimism led them to believe.

The 1942 vote showed practically no Republican gains in the East or South. There was apparently a 3- to 4-point gain, in terms of total votes cast in the Middle and Far West. The Republicans had made no noticeable headway among voters under forty years of age, and only slight gains among voters over forty. Most of their recruits appeared to be males. General prosperity in 1942 and the great reduction in persons on relief appeared to favor Republican candidates. While three out of every four voters on WPA voted Democratic in 1938 and 1942, actually very few remained on WPA in 1942, and as they returned to private occupations they apparently fell back into their usual political grooves —evidently not always Democratic.

At the next point in the New Deal tide, the 1944 election, the Democrats regained 21 seats, giving them 56 per cent of the two-party total. The fourth-term issue, accumulated dissatisfactions of three years of war, the failure of 7 or 8 million citizens to vote because most of them were in the armed forces abroad, concern over the President's health and his ability to survive a fourth term, the fact that the Republican platform supported a number of New Deal programs—these were among the general reasons why Roosevelt's proportion of the vote declined somewhat below that of 1940, and why the Democratic congressional gains in 1944 were relatively small. Democrats cast 54 per cent of the two-party popular vote for president compared with 55 per cent in 1940. The various economic classes and nationality groups lined up in the voting booths in 1944 about as in 1940, although there is evidence that the decline in isolationism favored the Democrats while a growing opposition among business and professional groups favored the Republicans.

In 1946 the Democrats finally lost control of both the House and the Senate. This was the lowest point in the New Deal tide, determined among other causes by a small turnout and by dissatisfaction with the hasty, confused, and erratic course of postwar decontrol, especially in the matter of prices. Two additional factors, charges of "communism" leveled against Democratic candidates, and a "hidden" depression in the midst of general prosperity, may also have played a part. For millions of people, the 1946 brand of prosperity actually meant a reduction in purchasing power from that of 1944–5 because of the sharp rise in prices following decontrol. The earnings of workers engaged in the durable-goods industries were further cut by the postwar reduction in hours worked, a cut not sufficiently offset by the wage-rate increases.

While the Democratic leaders were well aware of the significance and, from their standpoint, the necessity of a large turnout, very little was done in the 1946 campaign to ensure a heavy vote. Some of the most responsible Democratic leaders, while agreeing that the Republicans might gain, refused to acknowledge the possibility that they, the Democrats, might lose control of Congress. Millions of independent voters stayed away from the polls. The Republicans, on the other hand, apparently made great headway with the slogan: "Had Enough?—Vote Republican," so admirably expressive of the current postwar public temper. The ousting of former Vice President Henry Wallace, then Secretary of Commerce, from the Truman Cabinet over disagreement on foreign policy—at a crucial moment two months before the elections—deprived the Democratic Party of a vigorous campaigner needed to retain and keep alive the independent vote.

Instead of 43 million, which would have been normal, only 34 million citizens took part in the 1946 congressional elections. I estimate that about 7 million Democrats and 2 million Republicans failed to participate; that the majority of the 9 million were independents who preferred to indicate their temporary disapproval by staying home instead of voting the Republican ticket. The Republicans claimed millions had shifted to their side, but in view of the net reduction in the Republican vote it is difficult to see any substantial influx of Democrats to their ranks. In other words, the 1946 election, which finally shifted control of Congress from the Democrats to the Republicans, did not represent a landslide like the Democratic landslide of 1932. Contrary to Republican claims, it did not carry a popular mandate for Congress to depart from the New Deal programs—the kind of mandate the Democrats received when the Republicans were thrown out of office in 1932.

What do we see most clearly in this close-up view of the New Deal tide? One conclusion is fairly obvious. It is evident that the first half, the rising half, of the Democratic tide was largely a reaction against declining business activity and general economic distress. The declining half, on the other hand, was the aftermath of a series of different events, including business recession and war, the third- and fourth-term issues, and political apathy, particularly in the final phase from 1942 to 1946. The persistent appearance of business conditions and turnout as factors through the course of the tide now warrant a still closer view.

In this sharper focus we may observe the effect of the size of the vote and business conditions isolated from all other political elements. This I undertake to do presently. But there is another result of this review that is in the nature of a surprising discovery. The record of political tides, based on two-party strength in Congress, I first introduced into political discussions in 1938. I have examined it in great detail on numerous occasions ever since, but it was not until the winter of 1945, while trying to anticipate the outcome of the 1946 election, that I made the striking and highly useful observation that the New Deal political tide has actually been moving on a double track; on one level in years of presidential elections, and on another and lower one in the mid-term congressional elections. Thus observed, the New Deal tide stands out in the amazing simplicity shown in the next chapter.

Chapter 4:

The President's Coattail

The unanswered theological question of the Middle Ages: "How many angels can dance on the point of a needle?" has its counterpart in political discussion today: "How many Congressmen can ride into office on the president's coattail?" But this question we can answer definitely as a result of the discovery that the political tide is a duality.

The reader should look again at the irregular course of the New Deal tide, chart 4, based on congressional elections, and see how completely it is transformed into a smooth, dual curve in chart 5. This statistical magic may be easily explained. The key lies in the fact that congressional elections in mid-term are not strictly comparable with congressional elections in the more exciting presidential years. They must be studied separately. The congressional elections of 1928, 1932, 1936, 1940, and 1944 were part of presidential campaigns. They were influenced by the same national issues, personalities, and strategies that were the chief concern of both major parties in their efforts to elect their presidential candidates. In the mid-term elections, 1930, 1934, 1938, 1942, 1946, the congressional results were shaped by entirely different factors, largely local in character and lacking the nation-wide interest that prevails in presidential election years.

Presidential candidates tend to serve as lodestones, drawing voters to the support of the two major parties and sometimes to a predominant third party. There is greater uniformity in the conduct of presidential campaigns than of congressional campaigns by the two major parties in all sections of the country. The presidential candidates are the talk of all households, while Congressmen are of interest chiefly in their own districts. As a matter of fact, 30 to 40 per cent of the voters don't even know who their Congressmen are or what stand they have taken on any issue. Congressional elections do not have even the state-wide interest of senatorial elections. When only 60 to 70 per cent of the voters know the names of their Representatives in Congress, it is not surprising that, invariably, fewer voters participate in congressional than in presidential elections.

Let us turn again to the congressional tide in chart 5. Instead of zigzagging from one election to the next at two-year intervals (as in chart 4), the reader's eye follows a smooth curve connecting the results of 1928 with those of 1932, 1936, 1940, and 1944. If, with a second curve, we likewise connect the 1930 mid-term election results with those of 1934, 1938, and 1942, we find that the New Deal tide may be resolved into two components running parallel with each other. Democratic congressional strength in presidential years, as all good politicians know, is noticeably greater than in mid-term elections.

Whether caught up in the New Deal tide as an adherent or opponent, one must admit at least the pleasant smoothness of its course. Once it started upward, with the aid of the 1929–32 depression, the tide moved on a level of 6 to 7 percentage points higher in presidential than in mid-term election years. This suggests that in presidential campaigns 6 to 7 per cent of the 435 Democratic congressional candidates were elected mainly by virtue of the fact that they were on the national ticket. In other words, about 26 to 30 Congressmen thus appear to have ridden into office on the President's coattail in 1932, 1936, 1940, and 1944. It may also be said that about as many Democratic congressional candidates were defeated in each of the mid-term elections of 1930, 1934, 1938, and 1942 because they lacked presidential support.

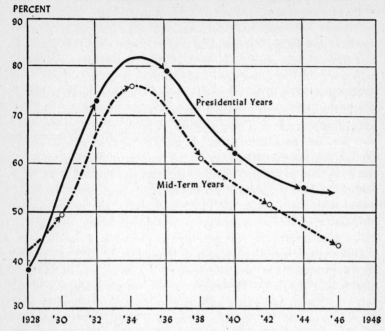

SOME CONGRESSMEN RIDE IN ON THE PRESIDENT'S COATTAIL

DEMOCRATIC PERCENTAGE OF TWO-PARTY MEMBERSHIP IN HOUSE
OF REPRESENTATIVES, 1928–46

More Democratic Congressmen are elected in years of presidential elections than in mid-term congressional election years. The difference is usually about 25 to 30 Congressmen.

CHART 5

This approach to the New Deal tide permits us to fix the date of its turning point quite accurately. It apparently came not between the 1936 and 1938 elections, but at some point between the 1934 and 1936 elections. The course of the dual tide suggests that if an election had been held in 1935, the Democrats would have seated a few more Congressmen than in 1934 or 1936.

The question will, of course, be asked whether the Republican tide in the 1920's and in earlier periods also had a dual character. This double track or zigzag feature of political swings has held true for the past fifty years. More Democratic congressional candidates, for example, won in the mid-term elections of 1922 and 1926 than in the presidential elections of 1924 and 1928. This is opposite to their experiences in the 1930's and 1940's, but consistent with them. As in the 1930's and 1940's, the congressional candidates of the party out of power fared better during the 1920's in mid-term than in presidential elections.

This analysis served admirably in the winter of 1945 in appraising the prospects for the 1946 election. It seemed a foregone conclusion that unless the Democrats could put on a vigorous campaign with men and issues adequate to the task of checking and possibly reversing the downward course of the New Deal tide, the Republicans were likely to take control of Congress. The Democratic congressional trend in the off years had by 1942 reached the low point of 51.5 per cent (as measured by seats in the lower house). But few political analysts, and few even among political leaders whose seats and committee assignments were imperiled, saw the danger so close at hand. They seemed to be misled by the fact that the 79th Congress, elected in 1944, was safely Democratic, and they reasoned that even if the Democrats lost a few seats, they would not lose control. What had happened in 1942, the last point on the midyear record applicable to 1946, seemed remote to them. They confused, as our chart so definitely makes plain, the tide in presidential election years with that of congressional years. Had they known that the power of the presidential coattail added 26 to 30 Democratic seats in 1944, and realized with what a handicap they entered the 1946 mid-term campaign lacking that support, they might have been more energetic in getting out the vote and answering effectively the Republican charges.

The downward trend of the political tide in the off years ending with 1942 quite accurately foretold the magnitude of the impending Democratic defeat in Congress. A simple projection of the tide to 1946 indicated that the Republicans would win 55 to 57 per cent of the seats, reducing the Democrats to 43 to 45 per cent. The Democrats actually elected only 43 per cent of their candidates, compared with 56 per cent in 1944.

This does not necessarily mean that the Republican victory in 1946 was inevitable. As we have seen, the course of the tide, on either its upper or its lower track, responds to economic conditions and political and social issues. In 1946 the Republicans didn't just bank on coming in on the outgoing Democratic tide. They added momentum by criticizing price controls, by capitalizing on apparent confusion in foreign policy as well as domestic reconversion, by calling some of their political opponents "communists," and by using catchy slogans. The early promise of a vigorous campaign, with strong men and strong issues to rouse public interest, did not materialize, and some Democratic candidates felt the times were so sharply against them that they feared their former allegiance to Roosevelt and his New Deal would be a detriment.

The absence of the presidential coattail, and the consequent loss of marginal Democratic Congressmen, were much more critical in 1946 than in 1938. In the presidential election of 1944 the Democrats won 21 more seats than in 1942, giving them a total of 243. They had 53 more seats than the Republicans, but a majority of only 25. This should have made it obvious that, lacking the advantage of a presidential coattail—usually worth 26 to 30 seats—the Democrats would lose control of Congress unless they could wage a vigorous campaign to get out the vote.

In 1938, when the Democrats controlled 333 seats, 79 per cent of the two-party total, the lack of presidential support had not been so important. With a comfortable margin of 115 seats over the minimum required for control (218), they could afford to lose the 26 to 30 Congressmen who had ridden in on Roosevelt's coattail in 1936. And while they actually lost many more because of the recession, their domination of Congress was not jeopardized.

Is there any difference between the pulling power of one president's coattail and that of another? My investigation has not gone far enough for a positive answer. The record does not indicate that Roosevelt's ability to help marginal Congressmen to victory was materially greater than Hoover's or Coolidge's. Undoubtedly the nation-wide ballyhoo and greater interest in the presidential race bring out more voters than in the less exciting midterm elections, and give certain congressional candidates the advantage of running on the ticket of the party in power. We are thus led to the conclusion that usually the power of the president's coattail is synonymous with increased voting interest and a greater turnout, a conclusion that will be further corroborated in the last chapter.

What does the double-track tide portend for the future? A great deal will depend on the trend of the presidential elections. Just as the take-off point for forecasting the 1946 election was the narrow and declining margin (1.5 per cent) by which the Democrats held control of the lower house in 1942, so the take-off point for judging the 1948 election is 1944, when 56 per cent of the Democratic congressional candidates won and the downward trend of the curve appeared to be flattening out. This meager evidence that the Democratic decline had definitely begun to taper off was soon corroborated by numerous congressional and mayoralty elections and public-opinion polls. By the end of 1947, for example, 56 per cent of the voting public indicated their preference for a Democratic president in 1948 and, as I will demonstrate in a later chapter, this meant that the Democratic tide during 1947 had risen again to the 1944 level.

All this suggests that the congressional elections in 1946 were affected by other factors in addition to the absence of a presidential coattail. Public-opinion polls and other indications suggest that the Democrats might have won 56 per cent of the House seats in 1947 had a presidential election been held then. The difference between this percentage and the 43 per cent obtained in 1946 represents about 55 seats, or twice the number we ascribe to the power of the president's coattail.

In other words, by separating the political tide into its two components and projecting both to 1947, it appears that in 1946 the Democrats lost about twice as many seats as they should have lost in a mid-term election. This, our next analysis will show, may have been due in large measure to an extraordinary lack of popular interest in the 1946 elections.

Chapter 5:

Ringing Doorbells

Many more doorbells than ever before are likely to be rung in coming elections. For the political campaign manager, getting out the vote is an old problem, but it wasn't until the 1942 congressional elections—when the Democrats came within 4 seats of losing control of the House—that concern over the size of the electorate became an important factor in campaign strategy. In that first war year neither major party made an unusual effort to stimulate interest in the election, and voting naturally fell off. The Republican turnout actually exceeded that of the Democrats for the first time since 1930, and the Republican gains in Congress came as an almost complete surprise, as did the general decline in voting. A still greater surprise was the almost equally light vote of 1946, which helped Republicans to take control of Congress.

Probably few citizens in mid-term congressional elections realize how much depends on whether they bestir themselves to go to the polls. Electing the right kind of Congress is fully as important as electing the right kind of president. Voting apathy can at times actually deprive a party of congressional control, or, more often, so reduce the operating margin as to affect the kind and course of legislation, or contribute to a stalemate in lawmaking by voting into power a Congress not in political harmony with the president.

In view of the role that numbers have played in the course of the New Deal tide, this chapter offers a bit of history relating to the growing interest in what is called turnout, and a simple method of estimating the normal turnout for the elections of 1948, 1950, and 1952.

On the strength of continued gains in local congressional and gubernatorial elections in the winter of 1943, the Republicans were making substantial claims of victory in 1944. The Democrats countered with the argument of Vice President Wallace in November 1942 that the Republican victories in that year were due to the fact that only about half as many persons as in 1940 took the trouble to vote. This was clearly an opportunity for making a factual analysis. A portion of my study was published in the *New Republic* in March 1944, under the timely title: "What Republican Trend?" Those who were aware of my anticipations for 1944, based on these findings, pointed out further that in the 1943 local elections participation had fallen off even more than in 1942, in some instances almost to the vanishing point. They took the position, later corroborated by the outcome of the 1944 election, that voter apathy in 1943–4 was obscuring the national trend; that a much larger vote in the presidential campaign would give the Democrats about the same strength as in 1940. Roosevelt actually received 54 per cent of the two-party vote, or only 1 per cent less than in 1940.

I found in my 1943–4 investigation that, in spite of differences in conditions, issues, and personalities, the reduction in turnout in practically all local elections since 1940 was associated with a decline in Democratic strength.

Political apathy was amazing even for local elections. In some cases, as in the Twenty-First Congressional District in New York City in March 1944, 80 to 90 per cent or more of those who had voted either Republican or Democratic in 1936 and 1940 stayed home. As a rule the stay-at-homes were more numerous among Democrats than Republicans, resulting in an increase in the Republican percentage of the two-party vote. But in view of the pronounced apathy evident among adherents of both parties, it could not be argued that many Democrats of 1940 had become Republicans.

As an example of the relation of turnout to Democratic strength, we may note what happened in a typical Midwestern district. The Second Congressional District in Kansas as usual elected the Republican candidate in a by-election early in 1943. The Democratic vote dropped from 63,000 in 1940 to less than 9,000 in 1943, a shrinkage of 85 per cent. The Republican vote also declined, but not so much as the Democratic. The Republican margin of victory thus increased substantially. Behind this appearance of a Republican trend, however, was nothing more than the sharp wartime decline in turnout.

Congressional Vote, Second District, Kansas, 1936–43

YEAR	TOTAL TWO-PARTY VOTE	PER CENT DEMOCRATIC
1936	132,000	45.5
1938	125,000	43.6
1940	136,000	46.0
1942	82,000	40.9
1943	29,000	31.0

With the increased interest in 1944, the vote in the Second Congressional District of Kansas rebounded to 116,000, and the Democrats increased their share to 41 per cent.

Size of Vote and Democratic Per cent, Up-State New York

YEAR	NUMBER VOTES CAST	PER CENT DEMOCRATIC
1936	2,800,000	45
1938	2,400,000	38
1940	3,100,000	42
1942	2,100,000	34
1943	1,800,000	32

A similar phenomenon was observed in New York State. In this case the record deals with the presidential elections of 1936 and 1940, the congressional elections of 1938, the gubernatorial election of 1942, and the election of lieutenant-governor in 1943. The Democratic share fell with the small turnout of 1938, rose with the larger vote of 1940, and declined in both the 1942 and the

1943 elections as the number of ballots cast shrank sharply. This repeats with great fidelity the Kansas experience. New York City and Albany, however, departed from the state pattern because voting behavior was fairly well stabilized in those areas, probably through efficient party organization. New York City went 75 per cent Democratic in 1936 and 65 per cent Democratic in 1938, and in spite of declining participation voted about 61 per cent Democratic in 1940, 1942, and 1943.

My survey contained a number of additional examples, including elections held in early 1944 in the Sixth District of Missouri, the First District of Colorado, the Second District of Oklahoma, and the Second and Seventeenth districts of Pennsylvania. These records showed consistently that the reduced turnout was the chief factor in the apparent decline of Democratic strength. Furthermore, they revealed that where apathy was most evident, the Democratic loss was greatest, as the following results in five 1944 elections before May 1 illustrate:

Five Special Off-Year Congressional Elections
(showing decline in participation and in Democratic per cent of two-party vote, 1942–4)

STATE AND DISTRICT		PER CENT DECLINE IN PARTICIPATION	PER CENT CHANGE DEMOCRATIC
Pennsylvania,	17th	−78	−20
New York,	21st	−66	−12
Pennsylvania,	2nd	−39	− 7
Colorado,	1st	−26	− 6
Oklahoma,	2nd	− 7	+ 4

In view of the statistical consistency of these records, I concluded that the Democrats might have elected their candidates in several 1943–4 local elections had more voters gone to the polls. Thus the Democratic candidate for lieutenant-governor in 1943 in New York might have won if an additional 30 per cent of the qualified electorate, or 1 million persons, had participated. Likewise, Democratic candidates for governor might have been elected in 1943 in New Jersey and Kentucky had the size of the vote been larger by 20 and 10 per cent respectively.

These straws foreshadowed reasonably well a Democratic victory in 1944. By combining them into a general index, I in-

THE SAW-TOOTH VOTE FOR REPUBLICAN AND DEMOCRATIC CONGRESSMEN

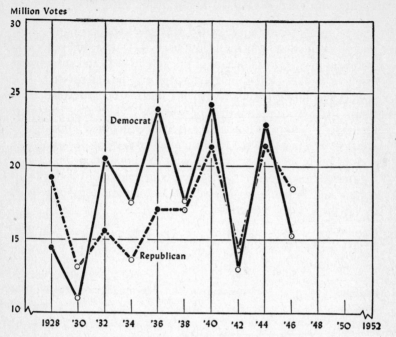

Million Votes

DEMOCRATIC AND REPUBLICAN VOTES CAST FOR CONGRESSMEN, 1928–46

The Democratic vote for congressmen usually falls off in mid-term elections much more than the Republican vote. Shrinkage in the 1942 and 1946 elections shows unusual mid-term apathy.

CHART 6

terpreted them to mean that the Democrats could win with 53 per cent of the two-party vote. Actually they won with 54 per cent.

It is not generally appreciated that participation in the 1944 and 1946 elections was far below normal. Unless this is seen in historical perspective, the size of the vote in 1948 and subsequent elections is likely to be underestimated and misinterpreted.

The fluctuating voting record for the ten congressional elections, 1928–46, supplies that perspective (chart 6). The most impressive feature in this curve is its saw-toothed appearance. Bearing in mind that the total number of persons of voting age rises in fairly regular proportion with the population, it is amazing to find how irregular is the number of votes cast for the Democratic and Republican tickets. The Democratic turnout reveals by far the greatest variations.

Decline in Votes between Presidential and Mid-Term Congressional Elections
(millions)

PERIOD	DEMOCRATIC	REPUBLICAN	TOTAL TWO-PARTY
1928–30	− 3.4	−6.2	− 9.6
1932–4	− 3.1	−2.0	− 5.1
1936–8	− 6.3	0	− 6.3
1940–2	−11.2	−7.2	−18.4
1944–6	− 7.0	−2.0	− 9.0
Average	− 6.2	−3.5	− 9.7

Except for 1942, when the two-party vote declined by 18 million, mid-term congressional elections recorded a shrinkage of 5 million to nearly 10 million ballots. The Democrats usually contributed the larger share of the decline. They accounted for practically all of it in 1938 and more than two thirds in 1946.

Similarly, in the presidential elections of the New Deal period the Democratic vote increased more than the Republican, 1940 being an exception.

To complete the voting picture, note that the combined votes cast by minor parties from 1928 to 1946 showed no such saw-tooth variations. In the aggregate they polled 2 per cent of the total vote in 1928 and 1944, reaching a maximum of 4.9 per cent in 1934. Between 1928 and 1936 their votes rose from about 630,-

000 to 1,940,000, and by 1944 declined to about 990,000. Minor-party strength is usually concentrated in a few states. In 1928 it was divided between the Farmer-Labor candidates of the North-west and Socialist candidates in the East. Nearly two thirds of the minor-party vote in 1944 was polled by the American-Labor and Liberal Party candidates in New York.

Increase in Votes between Congressional Mid-Term and Presidential Elections
(millions)

PERIOD	DEMOCRATIC	REPUBLICAN	TOTAL TWO-PARTY
1930–2	+9.5	+2.6	+12.1
1934–6	+6.5	+3.4	+ 9.9
1938–40	+2.5	+4.4	+ 6.9
1942–4	+9.9	+7.2	+17.1
Average	+7.1	+4.4	+11.5

The Democrats have been much more concerned than the Republicans about the size of the vote. Violent fluctuations in Democratic totals that contributed to their losses in 1942 and 1946 give ample justification for their greater interest in ringing doorbells to persuade voters to go to the polls.

Numbers in politics do not always have the same significance. During the 1932–8 phase of the New Deal tide, when the Democratic proportion in Congress exceeded 60 per cent, the decline in voting interest did not jeopardize their control but when their strength fell to 55 per cent or less, the effect of a small turnout could have been and in 1946 was fatal. This is shown in chart 7, where the total votes cast by all parties is contrasted with Democratic percentage of two-party membership in the House. The reader should note first the straight line drawn through the points representing the votes cast in the presidential elections of 1928, 1932, 1936, and 1940. The 1944 vote was clearly about 7 million short of the total called for by the rising trend.

The reader should next observe that I have drawn a curved line through the points in the upper half of the chart representing the Democratic membership in the House for the same four presidential elections. I did this to see what happened to the New Deal tide when the size of the vote was increasing normally, as indicated by the trend line in the lower part of chart 7. Having thus discovered the political trend that accompanied normal voting, we can now see how the falling off in participation is definitely and unmistakably reflected in the political tide. In every year of decline in the number of ballots cast (1930, 1934, 1938, 1942, and 1946), fewer Democratic congressional candidates were elected than was indicated by the New Deal tide for presidential years of normal voting.

How much the war effort kept people from voting in 1942 and 1944 is not generally appreciated, nor is the equally staggering political apathy of 1946. In previous mid-term elections (1930, 1934, and 1938) approximately 5 to 9 million fewer votes were cast for congressmen than in the preceding presidential years. In 1942 the total fell short by 22 million and in 1946 by about 20 million. In the intervening presidential election (1944) about 7 million eligible voters—most of them in the services—failed to vote. That failure probably cost the Democrats 4 million ballots, the Republicans 3 million. This was not disastrous to the Democrats, for the majority of their congressional candidates had the offsetting advantage of riding on the presidential coattail. In 1946 about 43 million persons should have participated in the congressional elections; only 34 million did. As we have seen, this cost the Democrats about 7 million votes and the Republicans only 2 million. Consequently the Democrats lost about twice as many seats as they would have lost under normal mid-term election conditions. By staying away from the polls, men and women who may have disapproved of the Democratic administration but didn't want to vote Republican helped unwittingly to bring the Republicans back into power in the Senate and House.

Many Congressmen, former, present, and future, would do well to examine the saw-tooth voting record of their districts in the 1930's and 1940's. Like former Congressmen Kopplemann of Connecticut or Biemiller of Wisconsin, they will find that it is possible to be voted in in presidential and out in mid-term election years because of the larger turnout for presidential elections, followed by apathy in mid-term congressional elections.

Political analysts, writing for popular consumption, seldom think in terms of normal. For that reason they quite often get themselves and their readers in trouble over figures and their meaning. Unless they study the records, as this book is intended

A SMALL VOTE DENTS A POLITICAL TIDE

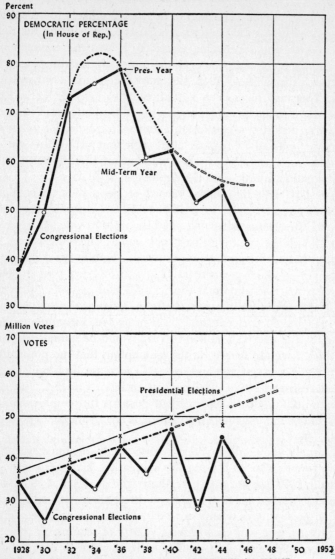

Percent

DEMOCRATIC PERCENTAGE
(In House of Rep.)

Pres. Year

Mid-Term Year

Congressional Elections

Million Votes

VOTES

Presidential Elections

Congressional Elections

1928 '30 '32 '34 '36 '38 '40 '42 '44 '46 '48 '50 1952

DEMOCRATIC PERCENTAGE OF TWO-PARTY MEMBERSHIP IN HOUSE OF REPRESENTATIVES AND NUMBER OF VOTES CAST FOR CONGRESSMEN AND PRESIDENT

Note how the mid-term falling off in the size of the vote for congressmen in 1930, 1934, 1938, 1942, 1946, was accompanied by a relatively smaller number of Democratic Congressmen elected (upper half of chart).

CHART 7

to encourage them and others to do, they are likely to accept the subnormal 1944 voting record as a basis for predicting the turn-out in 1948 and succeeding elections. It was the common but misleading practice to compare the unusually small registrations in 1946 with those of 1942, the most recent mid-term election year. This may have been logical, but not helpful, for in 1942 there was a pronounced depression in political interest. We arrive at just as distorted a conclusion about voting behavior when we compare political interest in 1946 with that of 1942 as we do about business conditions when we contrast the improved business situation in 1936 with the depression of 1932.

We start with the official record of population, twenty-one years of age and over, from 1920 to 1948 (including men and women, since women have also had the right to vote since World War I), and the number of past presidential votes. We see immediately that an increasing proportion of eligible voters has been participating—43.6 per cent in 1920 and 59.1 per cent in 1940. Disregarding the abnormal dip in 1944 and assuming that the rising interest in politics will continue, a figure of 62.5 per cent for 1948 and 64 per cent for 1952 is projected. Fifty-nine million votes in 1948 and 63.5 million in 1952 would be normal and reasonable, if we are correct in the assumption that the population twenty-one years of age and over will increase by 5 million between 1948 and 1952. (The population figures refer to July 1.)

Sixty million jobs is an excellent goal for full employment in 1950, but 60 million voters for 1948-52 is not an adequate political goal.

A turnout of 59 million voters in 1948 would, of course, surprise many people who do not see this tabulation. Sixty-three million voters in 1952 may surprise even those who do. Even if 59 million men and women go to the polls in 1948, there will still be 35 million persons over twenty-one years of age, most of them eligible to vote, who will abstain for a variety of reasons.

As for 1952, even if 80 million citizens were to cast ballots, there would still be nearly 20 million not exercising their obligations as citizens.

The congressional vote also is fairly easy to project, but not so easy to predict. We start by comparing the votes for congressmen and for president. In the 1928-44 elections two to three million fewer ballots were usually cast for congressmen than for president.

Population and Presidential Votes

YEAR	21 YEARS & OVER *Millions*	VOTES CAST *Millions*	PER CENT
1920	61.2	26.7	43.6
1924	65.9	29.1	44.2
1928	70.7	36.9	52.2
1932	75.4	39.8	52.8
1936	79.8	45.6	57.1
1940	84.3	49.8	59.1
1944	89.2	48.0	53.8
1948 *	94.2	(58.9)	(62.5)
1952 *	(99.2)	(63.5)	(64.0)

* Estimated.

Total Votes Cast for President and Congressmen
(millions)

YEAR	PRESI-DENT	CONGRESS-MEN	DIFFER-ENCE
1928	36.9	34.2	−2.7
1932	39.8	37.7	−2.1
1936	45.6	42.9	−2.7
1940	49.8	46.9	−2.9
1944	48.0	45.1	−2.9
Projection:			
1948	(58.9)	(55.9)	(−3.0)
1952	(63.5)	(60.3)	(−3.2)

By deducting approximately 3 million from the projections for the presidential votes, it appears that the minimum goal for doorbell-ringers should be far above the turnout of 1946. If 56 million votes for congressmen in 1948 and 60 million in 1952 can be considered normal, then the goals for presidential candidates should be set much higher. For mid-term elections, estimates of normal turnout can be approximated by noting that in 1934 the congressional vote was about 80 per cent of the turnout in the previous presidential election; in 1938 only 75 per cent. This suggests a goal of at least 47 million votes for 1950—13 million more than in 1946.

Three final precautionary observations are called for at this point. I have said little about the reasons for the tendency of the Democratic percentage of votes cast to decline with a falling off in participation. There are some studies, such as that of Anderson and Davidson on *Ballots and the Democratic Class Struggle in California,* that indicate greater political apathy among low-income groups (who constituted the backbone of the Democratic Party in the New Deal tide) than among higher-income groups. This is probably the most reasonable explanation. It does not necessarily mean, however, that in larger metropolitan areas, such as New York City and Chicago, apathy is greater among working-class Democrats than business and professional and other higher-income groups. I have already noted that in the New York elections of 1940, 1942, 1943, and 1944 the variations in the total vote cast did not alter the balance between the two major parties.

There are other instances, relatively unimportant in the over-all national picture discussed in this chapter, where the size of the vote has just the opposite relation to party strength to what is generally the case. In the South, for example, very few Republicans vote in congressional elections, probably because the predominance of Democrats leaves little doubt of the outcome. This results in an increase in the Democratic percentage, instead of the usual decrease noted elsewhere. Unless these different conditions in the border and Southern states are recognized, there may be misleading interpretations of the results of campaigns to get out the vote.

As an illustration we have the congressional election in Baltimore in 1947. Here Democrats and labor leaders claimed that the very high percentage of the two-party vote cast for their candidates was indicative of the response to their efforts to arouse voting interest. Actually a very high Democratic percentage was to be expected in a light by-election vote in a predominantly Democratic border-state district. Conversely, in rural Kansas and rural New York, certainty of Republican victories in mid-term elections induces relatively greater apathy among Democratic than Republican voters. These departures from the general national pattern call for deeper probing into the real reasons for political apathy and its effect on the fortunes of the two major parties than has been done so far.

From a practical standpoint, then, the size of the vote is of greatest concern to both Republicans and Democrats in mid-term congressional elections, and particularly in districts where the two parties are almost evenly matched. From a national standpoint, turnout is of primary concern in years when either party has a majority of, say, less than 10 per cent of the seats in the House (as was the case in 1942–6) and the usual decline in voting can precipitate a change in control. On the other hand, ground lost in mid-term elections is usually regained in the suc-ceeding campaign as a result of invariably increased participation and the power of a winning presidential candidate to carry mar-ginal congressmen to victory. In the future as in the past, varia-tions in the size of the vote may be expected—on the average—to be relatively unimportant compared with business fluctuations and third-party developments. However, if we learn to master the business cycle, thus reducing its impact on the political cycle, the role of numbers and the ringing of doorbells will tend to increase in campaign strategy.

Chapter 6:

When Business Cycle Meets Political Cycle

One of the indoor political sports after the 1946 election was to pose two questions on business and political prospects. One was: "Whom would the voting public blame if a depression occurred in 1948—the Democrats or the Republicans?" The other: "If the Republicans win in 1948, will a depression in 1952 bring the Democrats back?" One would think that after all the economic and political gyrations this country has experienced both questions could be readily answered, even though the first primarily involves voter response and the second a long-range forecast of the business cycle. Yet these are difficult questions for anyone to tackle, whether statesman, politician, statistician, or average voter. I intend to toss both of them to the reader, but not until I have supplied a few hints on the relation of the business cycle to the political tide, and on what course the business cycle may be expected to take during this postwar decade, if experience after other wars offers an analogy.

The business cycle, by which I mean the fluctuations in indus-

50

trial production and employment, outweighs in political importance changes in the size of the vote. This generalization appears
to hold not only for the period covered by the New Deal tide but
also for the past hundred years. In the long-time political record
we have found that business depressions are of primary importance in producing changes in party control.

Business depressions played a powerful role in throwing the
Republicans out of office in 1874, after 1908, and in 1932, and
they had exactly the same influence in ousting the Democrats
after the panic of 1858 and during the economic setbacks of
1894 and 1920. These were major political upheavals and major
business depressions.

Franklin D. Roosevelt was a depression-created President—the
Democratic ticket in 1932 was bound to win in view of the nation-
wide distress and dissatisfaction. Harding in 1920, McKinley in
1896, and Cleveland in 1884 were also depression-made Presidents. Had the deciding electoral vote been cast for the candidate
who had the majority of the popular vote in 1876, Tilden, too,
would have been a depression-made president.

The entire rise in the Democratic curve from 1928 to 1936
(chart 8) I have already traced to the great depression of
1929–32, and to the large volume of unemployment that prevailed
in 1932–6. The first major reversal in the New Deal tide came in
1938 with the decline in business activity and agricultural prices
and the rise in unemployment.

This apparently clear relation between business recessions and
political behavior needs to be taken into account in appraising
the various reasons generally given for the Democratic loss of
congressional membership in 1938. The most commonly heard
explanations were in terms of policies pursued by the New Deal
after the 1936 election. These explanations, as already indicated,
included displeasure over the efforts to pack the Supreme Court,
attempts made by New Deal executives to influence state elections, dissatisfaction with the WPA standards of wages and work
—particularly criticized by farmers and other rural people—and
disapproval of the administration's apparent attitude toward the
C.I.O. sit-down strikes in 1937. It is quite likely, however, that
no one, perhaps not even all, of these factors contributed so
much to the Democratic loss of seats in 1938 as the sharp setback
in business. Industrial activity, factory payrolls, and farm prices

fell with record-breaking speed. Between March and December 1937 industrial production fell off 30 per cent and factory payrolls and farm prices about 20 per cent. There was little improvement during the first part of 1938.

This downturn in the economic cycle undoubtedly offers a more likely explanation of the first decline in New Deal Democratic political power than the various other reasons given at the time.

Business activity does not appear to have been influential in the congressional losses sustained by the Democrats in 1942, but I am inclined to think that part of the setback in 1946 (a setback leading to the loss of control in both Senate and House) was unquestionably the result of economic conditions. As I have already pointed out, millions of voters—particularly those whose incomes had remained stable—were beginning to feel keenly the shrinkage in purchasing power as food prices rose sharply in 1946. Mounting food costs take the greatest toll from the workers' pay envelopes. Farmers, on the other hand, gained, or at least did not lose, in the 1946 inflation. By October 1946, living costs had risen about 20 per cent above those of 1944, and the shrinkage in factory workers' real purchasing power—particularly of those in the heavy-goods industries—amounted to 20 per cent or more.

The political repercussion of this loss of purchasing power appears in the fact that, while the Republicans gained less than 3 percentage points in the 1946 popular vote in 10 predominantly agricultural states, they gained 4 to 10 points in states where heavy-goods industries are located: Rhode Island, Connecticut, New York, Delaware, Pennsylvania, Ohio, Illinois, and Michigan. The Republicans gained most ground in areas where living costs, combined with reduced earnings, hurt most. They won about 55 lower-house seats in the urban areas when normally they might have added 25 seats in a mid-term election.

While wide swings in the political tide are due primarily to sharp reversals in business conditions, the minor swings are brought about by at least two factors: business activity and political apathy. Sometimes they work together; sometimes, working in opposite directions, they offset each other.

To measure the relation of business activity and mid-term apathy to the political tide, we need a longer record of experience than that covered by the New Deal. Furthermore, for studies in political behavior we lack an adequate measure of business activ-

A BUSINESS DEPRESSION REVERSES A POLITICAL TIDE

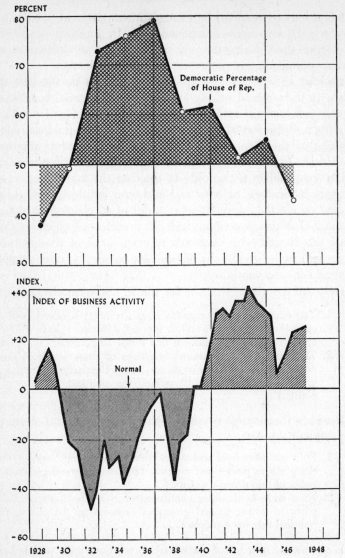

PERCENT

Democratic Percentage
of House of Rep.

INDEX OF BUSINESS ACTIVITY

Normal

1928 '30 '32 '34 '36 '38 '40 '42 '44 '46 1948

DEMOCRATIC PERCENTAGE OF TWO-PARTY MEMBERSHIP IN HOUSE OF REPRESENTATIVES AND BUSINESS ACTIVITY

The business depression of 1930 and 1932 started the upward phase of the New Deal tide, and the depression of 1938 initiated its downward phase. (Index of business activity for June and October, Cleveland Trust Co.)

CHART 8

ity. Is it best represented by changes in employment, income, or production? Are voters influenced more by business conditions at election time, during the year or two before an election, or by a change immediately preceding a particular election?

Lacking answers to these questions, we must do the best we can with the material readily available. That material consists of an index of business activity for October of each year from 1854 to date, and the record of the Democratic and Republican composition of the House. The business index represents physical production in relation to what the statistician considers normal. Since our problem is twofold—to discover the average effect of changes in business activity and mid-term political apathy—let us first divide the entire 92-year record of 46 elections into two groups. One group contains the 23 presidential elections, the other the 23 mid-term elections. In each, some of the elections were held under conditions of business prosperity, others under adverse business conditions.

Here are the average results for the 23 mid-term elections:

1. Ten occurred under conditions of declining business, and in each the party in power lost ground. (Business down 13 percentage points, the political tide down 15 points.)
2. Thirteen were held under conditions of rising levels of business, and in all but one of those (1934) the party in power lost ground. (Business up 10 points, the political tide down 8 points.)

Here are the average results for the 23 congressional elections in presidential years:

1. Fourteen were held under conditions of declining business, and the party in power lost ground. (Business down 9 points, the political tide down 4 points.)
2. Nine were held under conditions of rising business, and the party in power gained ground. (Business up 13 points, the political tide up 4 points.)

With the aid of a bit of statistical correlation, with which I do not need to bother the reader, these four sets of facts permit the following generalizations. If business activity remains unchanged between a presidential and an off-year election, normal political apathy causes the party in power to lose about 8 per cent of the two-party membership in the lower house, or 35 seats. (This is approximately comparable with the power credited to the president's coattail.) In a mid-term election, the losses of the dominant party might be checked and cut in half if business activity has advanced 20 points since the previous election, or the losses might be doubled if business has declined 20 points. If the business index remains unchanged between presidential elections, the party in power neither gains nor loses, but an advance of 20 points tends to give that party 35 to 40 additional seats. A similar decline in business tends to shift that many seats to the opposition.

These generalizations cannot, of course, be expected to apply to any one year like 1948, 1950, or 1952, for they are derived from experience over a period in which the relation of business alone to the political tide varied considerably. Other factors besides the business situation have influenced elections in the past, and will in the future. It is safe, however, to predict that if business conditions remain at the 1948 level—which is above that of 1946—the party that will be considered to be in power will gain more seats in 1948 than in 1946, and more in 1952 than in 1950.

But which party will be considered as being in power? With both Houses of Congress under Republican control in 1947–8,

Relation of Business Recessions to Mid-Term Congressional Elections

YEAR	PER CENT CHANGE IN BUSINESS ACTIVITY [1]	PER CENT CHANGE IN MAJOR PARTY HOUSE MEMBERSHIP	MAJOR PARTY
1858	−14	−13	D
1862	− 3	− 3	R
1870	− 7	−13	R
1874	−18	−33	R
1894	−10	−33	D
1914	−18	−14	D
1918	− 7	− 5 [2]	D
1930	−30	−11	R
1938	−14	−16	D
1946	− 9	−12	D
Average	−13	−15	

[1] Changes in the Cleveland Trust Company Index of Business Activity between October of the given year and October two years earlier.
[2] While the Republicans in 1916 had a 1-point House majority, the administration in power was considered Democratic.

will citizens assume that they are voting for or against a Republican administration even though the Democrats control the presidency? For a parallel, political analysts often turn to the post World War situation just preceding 1920. Then, the House and Senate were also preponderantly Republican, while Woodrow Wilson, a Democrat, was President. He and his party were defeated in 1920.

Relation of Business Recessions to Congressional Elections in Presidential Years

YEAR	PER CENT CHANGE IN BUSINESS ACTIVITY [1]	PER CENT CHANGE IN MAJOR PARTY HOUSE MEMBERSHIP	MAJOR PARTY
1856	−10	− 7	R
1868	− 8	− 4	R
1876	− 5	− 8	D
1884	−18	− 7	D
1892	− 7	− 8	D
1896	−12	−11	R
1900	− 4	+ 4	R
1904	− 8	+11	R
1908	−21	− 2	R
1920	−13	−14 [2]	D
1924	− 2	+ 5	R
1928	− 1	+ 7	R
1932	−20	−24	R
1944	− 3	+ 3	D
Average	−10	− 5	

[1] Changes in the Cleveland Trust Company Index of Business Activity between October of the given year and October two years earlier.

[2] While Republicans controlled the Congress elected in 1918, the administration in power was considered Democratic.

But before accepting the 1920 election as an analogy we must bear in mind that Wilson's defeat was as much the result of a business depression as of the conflict over the League of Nations issue. By November 1920 the domestic agricultural and industrial depression was already well under way. Prices received by farmers for their products had declined 20 per cent between May and November 1920, and industrial production had fallen by 15 per cent. The Democrats lost ground in all states.

It is the nation-wide character of the 1920 political reaction, typical of depression years, that leads us to assume that the public generally considered the 1919–20 administration as Democratic and held Woodrow Wilson responsible for the economic setback; this in spite of the fact that the Republicans controlled both the House and Senate.

A domestic economic crisis, affecting all states and all industries, is more likely to produce a common political response than an international issue. International crises cause regional cleavages in sympathies and in politics, but a major business depression affects all groups and sections with common adversity.

Our economy is in a literal sense a political economy, as is demonstrated from time to time when we change our political horses in the midstream of business depressions. Of the seven presidential elections since 1918, two were held in periods of deflation and depression, 1932 and 1920. These are the only two since World War I in which every state in the Union shifted position. In 1932 the Democratic vote was larger in every state than in 1928. In 1920 the Republican vote in every state was larger than in 1916. In the same way, many expected every state to shift toward the Republican side if the 1948 elections were held in an atmosphere of tobogganing prices and slackening production, except for one major difference. In 1920 the League of Nations issue dominated political discussion, and domestic economic distress received less political attention. A similar business development in 1948 or 1950 would receive greater attention. Given the bipartisan approach to foreign policy, political discussion would center on domestic problems. There would be open and lively discussion whether to lay the blame for the depression on the Democratic President, the Republican majority, or the Democratic minority in Congress. Domestic distress would sway the election, but not necessarily in favor of the Republicans.

Historical analogy can never be very conclusive. A more helpful answer to the question whether a depression in the fall of 1948 would be charged to the Democrats or the Republicans was contained in public-opinion polls available during the last half of 1947. They showed that the Democratic Party had regained popularity since the 1946 elections and had, in fact, made headway in putting more of the blame for rising prices on Republican Congressmen and Senators who helped to destroy price control in 1946.

The importance of the business cycle in shaping the next phase of the political tide makes it necessary to give some consideration to the economic conditions that may be expected to prevail in 1948, 1950, and 1952, even if what we say boils down to nothing more than an honest: "I don't know."

It is as difficult to predict what course the business cycle will follow in the immediate future as to give a long-range forecast. Many business executives and a number of economists in private industry and government find their batting averages uncomfortably low. What business executives thought of the economic outlook early in 1947 and at the beginning of 1948 is shown in the Elmo Roper polls. To the question: "We'd like to know how you feel about the general business outlook for 1948. In comparing it to 1947, which of the following do you expect?" the following distribution of answers was obtained:

	May 1947 PER CENT	January 1948 PER CENT
Those who expected—		
A sharp upturn	1	1
A moderate upturn	9	20
No appreciable change	16	39
A moderate downturn	67	37
A sharp downturn	7	2
No estimate		1
Total	100	100

The striking fact in the 1947 survey is the large proportion (74 per cent) of executives who expected a downturn, which didn't materialize.

We find a distinct change of sentiment when we compare the answers in the two surveys. Optimism doubled, pessimism decreased noticeably. With so large a proportion of failure in their forecasts in 1947, the estimates of business executives for 1948 can be regarded as little more than an interesting exercise, certainly not a basis for judging what the business situation is likely to be in the month or quarter preceding an election.

Economists who expected a depression by the end of 1947 also revised their forecasts. First they set the coming depression forward to the last half of 1948, but then in the light of military expenditures anticipated for 1948-9, tax reductions, and the 1948-52 Marshall foreign aid program the date of the expected depression was set forward indefinitely. As a matter of fact, no one knows when to expect a recession or depression. No one can know how soon or at what speed dangerously inflated prices will return to a stable level. Will good crops, or a consumer strike, or congressional action start the decline? Not even the three experienced men chosen by the President to serve as his Council of Economic Advisers and their twelve assistants, whose daily concern is with the future course of production, employment, income, prices, and purchasing power, can draw for us with any degree of certainty the employment-production-price line of the next few years. We all have hopes and fears, depending on the extent of our experience and knowledge and the strength of our confidence in the wisdom of Congress, labor, management, and agricultural leaders to keep the economic machinery going at top speed. As for predicting an exact date for the next depression, the intelligent reader can probably give as good a guess as the economist, statistician, businessman, or government official. If he doubts this, let him look carefully at the following record and he will soon find himself in the front line with the best of business forecasters.

When in doubt about the future, it is often good to look at the past, particularly that part of the past which is most pertinent. It is also wise to take neither that past nor oneself too seriously. With this admonition, the reader may note the course of business during the first decade after the Civil War, after World War I, and so far since World War II.

The first year after the Civil War, 1865, brought a boom; then came a depression in 1867. Revival and prosperity in 1869–70 were followed by a recession in 1871, and the good years gave way to a real financial panic and a deep and prolonged depression in 1873–4. The depression of 1867–8 cost the Republicans 4 per cent of the seats in Congress; that of 1870, 13 per cent; 1872, a boom year, saw a revival, but when the Republicans lost 33 per cent of the seats in 1874, the Democrats took over.

The course taken by business and politics after World War I was quite like that of the post Civil War decade, allowing for some difference in timing. Just as in 1865, we had a boom in the year after the war, 1919. Just as in 1867, two years after the boom we had a depression in 1921. Then, as in 1869–70, came prosperity in 1923 and a mild setback in 1924. After 1924 it took five

Timetable of Postwar Business and Political Cycles

YEAR	STATE OF BUSINESS	CHANGE IN PO-LITICAL TIDE [1]	YEAR	STATE OF BUSINESS	CHANGE IN PO-LITICAL TIDE	YEAR	STATE OF BUSINESS	CHANGE IN PO-LITICAL TIDE
1864	War prosperity	+19	1918	War prosperity, recession	-5	1945	War prosperity, recession	
1865	Boom, recession		1919	Revival, prosperity		1946	Recession, prosperity	-11
1866	Mild depression	-2	1920	Prosperity, depression	-14	1947	Prosperity	
1867	Depression		1921	Depression		1948		
1868	Revival	-4	1922	Revival, prosperity	-17	1949		
1869	Prosperity		1923	Prosperity, recession		1950		
1870	Recession, mild depression	-13	1924	Mild depression, revival	+5	1951		
1871	Revival, prosperity		1925	Prosperity		1952		
1872	Prosperity	+12	1926	Prosperity	-2	1953		
1873	Prosperity, panic, recession		1927	Mild recession		1954		
1874	Depression	-33	1928	Revival, prosperity	+7	1955		
1875	Depression		1929	Prosperity, panic, recession		1956		
1876	Depression	-9	1930	Depression	-11	1957		
1877	Depression		1931	Depression		1958		
1878	Depression, revival	-2	1932	Depression, revival	-24	1959		

[1] Change in percentage of major-party membership in House of Representatives.

60

years to produce the peak of the financial boom and collapse of 1929, whereas after 1870 it took only three years until the collapse of the speculative boom of 1873. Unless one is a stickler for exact parallels, and of course one shouldn't be, these two simple records should be more than amusing.

Since World War II ended, in 1945, we have had the typical letdown from the wartime peak of production and the early postwar prosperity of 1947. From here on, the reader may either fill in the last column in the table on page 60 with his own guesses, let his favorite forecaster do it for him, or, perhaps best of all, let time do it. Apparently, if we are to have a major postwar depression like those of 1921 and 1867, it has been somewhat delayed. To fulfill the expectations of most students of postwar business cycles, including many businessmen as well as economists, it should have arrived in 1948. Perhaps a delayed reaction might have been a more reasonable expectation if it had been borne in mind that World War II exceeded World War I in intensity, duration, and devastation or if the 1948-9 increase in military expenditures so soon after VJ-Day could have been anticipated.

With one reservation, this is probably as far as we can go in projecting the business cycle. If and when a depression develops that may be considered the equivalent of the 1921 and 1867 setbacks, it may be possible to fall back on one of the most common characteristics of American business cycles: their tendency to run in roughly three- to four-year minor swings from one low point to the next and, after two or three such relatively short movements, to develop into major depressions. These are the cycles that the Employment Act of 1946, creating the Council of Economic Advisers and the Joint Committee on the Economic Report, was intended to iron out. If we succeed in leveling the peaks and valleys of business activity or, better still, could prevent the 1948 boom from being followed ultimately by a comparable bust, the next political cycle will fluctuate less widely than the one portrayed in the last chapter.

Chapter 7:

The Power of Third Parties

Third parties of any real magnitude have rarely left a dent in the course of the Democratic-Republican tide since the Civil War. Nevertheless, though they have not elected their presidential candidates, their influence can be traced as a continuous chain through the political cycles of the past century.

The two outstanding third-party movements in recent decades, Theodore Roosevelt's Bull Moose Party in 1912 and the elder LaFollette's Progressive Party in 1924, were intimately related in personalities and programs. Henry Wallace's third party launched in 1948 is not entirely unlike LaFollette's. In fact, it was the Progressive movement of 1910–11, with LaFollette as the center of interest, that was diverted by friends of Theodore Roosevelt into the Bull Moose Party of 1912. Some of these Progressives and followers of Theodore Roosevelt showed up twenty-two years later as supporters of the LaFollette anti-monopoly and peace platform. Shortly after announcing his decision to seek the presidency, Henry Wallace in his article on "Third Parties and the American Tradition" in the *New Republic* for January 19, 1948 referred to the LaFollette platform as the *perfect parallel* for the party he hoped to lead in the 1948 campaign and said: "Today it is only necessary to change the year 1924 to 1948 and the words 'American people' to 'people of the entire world.'"

The 1924 third party thus takes on added significance and will be examined in the last half of the chapter in some detail for the suggestive light it sheds on the probable size of the Wallace vote and what states will give him the greatest and which the least support. How effectively a third party could divert electoral votes in 1948 from the Democratic column to the Republican will be shown in a later chapter.

An important fact about third parties likely to be overlooked is that they have not had the same influence on congressional as on presidential elections. Unlike business depressions and voting apathy, which can alter the shape and course of either a congressional or a presidential political tide, third-party movements affect primarily the presidential. This could have special significance in 1948, 1950, and 1952. Not since 1860 have minor parties elected a substantial number of congressional candidates. Even in 1912, when Theodore Roosevelt received 27 per cent of the popular vote, the two major parties elected all but 18, or 96 per cent, of the 435 Congressmen. In 1924, when LaFollette received 17 per cent of the vote, the two major parties won all but 5, or 99 per cent, of the seats in the House. Certainly in the early stages of a third-party movement its chief influence is on the outcome of the presidential race. At the beginning of 1948, when there was already ample evidence that the Republicans had lost some, if not all, the congressional ground gained in 1946, the central question raised by the prospect of a third party was whether it might not help elect a Republican president at the same time that a Democratic majority was returned to Congress.

Let us now note what a third party can do to a presidential political tide as illustrated in chart 9. The Democratic proportion of the two-party vote for president from 1896 to 1944 is shown by the solid line and the percentages of the entire vote by the dotted line. At certain points, particularly 1912 and 1924, there is substantial divergence. In 1912, while Wilson polled only 42 per cent of the total vote, he received 64 per cent of the two-party vote, and that gave him the election.

These discrepancies of 22 points in 1912 and 5 points in 1924, however, do not tell us exactly what we want to know. They merely indicate that a third party of some importance, like that of 1912, can alter the contour—not the course—of a political tide. For most purposes in this book we shall find the two-party rather than three-party vote for president most serviceable, as will be seen presently when we try to determine from which of the major parties a third draws its strength. I shall, incidentally, use the two-party record as a standard for comparing the voting characteristics of the several states with those of the nation. There we shall see mirrored in the individual state records the easily remembered key points of chart 9, the twin Democratic peaks of 1912 and 1936 (twenty-four years apart), and bottoms of 1904 and 1924 (twenty years apart).

In view of the rise of third-party interest in 1948, it is instructive to know how many votes Senator LaFollette's Progressives in 1924 drew from the Democratic candidate, John W. Davis, and how many from the Republican, Calvin Coolidge. How many votes did Theodore Roosevelt's Bull Moose Party take in 1912 from President Taft, the Republican candidate, and how many from the Democrats? It is usually assumed that Roosevelt diverted enough votes from the Republicans to throw the election to Woodrow Wilson, just as Breckenridge in 1860 is assumed to have divided Democratic strength sufficiently to elect Lincoln. From what follows, there is reason to believe that this interpretation gives Roosevelt's third party too much credit.

To estimate the influence of third parties on presidential elections, we must remember that congressional elections are not materially affected by such movements. By establishing the normal relation between the number of congressmen elected by a major party, and the percentage of the two-party popular vote cast for its presidential candidate, we can estimate the number of votes drawn from each party by the newcomer. This procedure of course assumes that the third party puts only a few of its own congressional candidates in the field.

The relationship we are here concerned with is evident in chart 3, where the long-time record of the two-party popular vote for president is contrasted with the similar record of House membership. For the period during which that relationship was closest, 1900 to 1944, it may be shown more clearly by the fol-

CHART 9

THE POLITICAL PATTERN

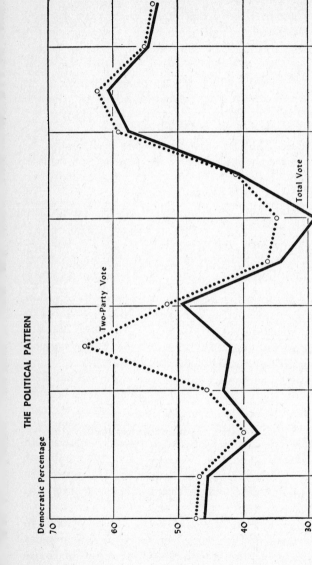

Democratic Percentage

DEMOCRATIC PERCENTAGE OF THE TWO-PARTY AND THE TOTAL VOTE CAST FOR PRESIDENT, 1896–1944.

The two records show the same contours, except when the 1912 and 1924 third parties caused them to deviate. The pattern shows two peaks, 1912 and 1936, and two bottoms, 1904 and 1924.

lowing table and chart 10. Since members of the lower house and
the president are both elected by popular vote, there should be a
close correspondence between the Democratic percentage of the
two-party vote and the proportion of all Democratic congressional candidates elected by that popular vote. Discrepancies between them must, therefore, be the result of particular causes,
such as the appearance of a third party or, as in 1940, the third-
term issue. Because the South is always predominantly Democratic and, as a rule, elects congressmen by a relatively smaller
vote than is cast in other states, the correspondence between our
two columns of figures in the table given below is not exact,
though quite close. Thus between the bottom of 1920 and the
peak of 1936 the Democratic share of the popular vote rose 26
percentage points; the comparable rise in the congressional percentage was 48 points, almost twice as much.

The exact relationship, however, is best shown if these two
sets of figures are presented in a chart where the reader can see
at a glance—provided it is not an impatient glance—that the
greater the Democratic share in the popular vote for president,
the greater the Democratic share in House membership
(chart 10).

Two major facts stand out. The first is that party membership
in the House is more variable than its share in the popular vote;

*Relation between Democratic Per cent of Two-Party Membership
in the House and the Popular Vote for President*

YEAR	DEMOCRATIC PER CENT IN HOUSE	DEMOCRATIC PER CENT OF POPULAR VOTE FOR PRESIDENT	DIFFERENCE
1920	30.6	36.1	+5.5
1928	37.9	41.2	+3.3
1924	42.6	34.8	−7.8
1900	43.6	46.8	+3.2
1908	44.0	45.5	+1.1
1916	49.3	51.7	+2.4
1944	55.0	53.8	−1.2
1940	60.8	55.0	−5.8
1912	69.5	64.4	−5.1
1932	72.8	59.1	−13.7
1936	78.9	62.2	−16.7

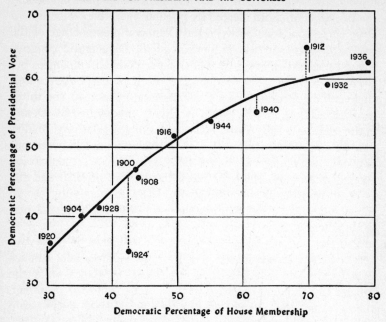

THE VOTE FOR PRESIDENT AND HIS CONGRESS

Democratic Percentage of Presidential Vote (vertical axis)

Democratic Percentage of House Membership (horizontal axis)

RELATION OF DEMOCRATIC PERCENTAGE OF TWO-PARTY VOTE FOR PRESIDENT AND DEMOCRATIC PERCENTAGE OF HOUSE MEMBERSHIP

A 60 per cent Democratic popular vote for president usually elects two thirds or more of the Democratic candidates. But a 40 per cent vote elects about a third of them. The low presidential vote of 1924 indicates that the La-Follette third party drew heavily from the Democrats.

CHART 10

that is, as Democratic membership in the House rises from 30 to 40 per cent, the party's share of the popular vote for president goes from 34 to 44 per cent (in each case a 10-point change), but when the Democratic percentage in the House moves beyond that point, the popular vote does not keep pace. A 10-point rise from 70 to 80 per cent in House membership is accompanied by an additional 1.5 points in the presidential vote.

The second is that three years, 1912, 1924, and 1940, do not fit the curve. Because they do not fit, we can learn something from them about third parties and, in the case of 1940, about the opposition to the Roosevelt third term.

According to the usual relation between the congressional and presidential tides, 69 per cent of the Democratic candidates for Congress are elected when the popular two-party vote for president is 59 per cent Democratic; not, as in 1912, 64 per cent. This normal Democratic figure, 59 per cent, indicates how the total vote cast for the three parties would have been divided among Democrats and Republicans had there been no Bull Moose movement.

If the 13,900,000 votes cast in 1912 for the three parties had been 59 per cent Democratic and 41 per cent Republican, Wilson might have polled 8,200,000 and Taft 5,700,000 votes. Since the Democrats actually won about 2,000,000 less and Taft also about 2,200,000 less, we must assume that Roosevelt drew about the same number of votes from each party.

Between 1908 and 1912 the total Democratic vote remained practically unchanged—6,400,000 in 1908 and nearly 6,300,000 in 1912—but the Republicans dropped from 7,679,000 to 3,484,000. It is generally assumed, therefore, that Roosevelt's following came entirely from the Republican side and so brought about Taft's defeat and Wilson's victory.

If our analysis yields a more balanced picture of what happened, as it probably does, Wilson would have been elected even if Roosevelt had not run. The LaFollette party in 1924 drew its followers almost entirely from among the Democrats, but couldn't have won the election even if all the Democratic votes had swung to its side. In that year, when 43 per cent of the Democratic candidates for the House were elected, the popular vote for president should have been divided 45 per cent Democratic and 55 per cent Republican. The three parties polled nearly 29,000.-

000 votes, which in a two-party campaign should have given 15,915,000 to the Republicans and 13,025,000 to the Democrats. Actually Democratic candidate Davis received only 8,381,000 votes or about 4,600,000 short, while Coolidge won 15,725,000, or about the number to be expected. The various progressive, liberal, and socialist groups, who would have voted Democratic in a two-party campaign, probably supplied practically all of La-Follette's 4,826,000 votes.

Let us now digress for a moment and make use of this basic relation between House membership and popular vote for president to evaluate how many votes the third-term issue cost Franklin D. Roosevelt in 1940. We must not take it for granted that those opposed to a third term would necessarily vote against congressmen running on the Roosevelt ticket. While we cannot state with finality the strength of opposition to the third term, we can formulate a fair estimate.

The popular vote that in 1940 elected 62 per cent of the Democratic candidates for the House should, according to chart 10, have given Roosevelt 57.5 per cent of the two-party total in 1940; instead he received 55 per cent. Therefore it may be estimated that the third-term issue cost Roosevelt a maximum of about 2.5 per cent of nearly 50 million votes, or, allowing for a margin of doubt in our formula, 1 to 1.5 million.

The fourth-term issue does not appear to have played an observable part in the 1944 election. It probably was offset and lost among other minor issues.

The importance of third parties in determining the outcome of an election obviously depends on which of the major parties bears the brunt of the defection. In 1912 the political tide was running strongly liberal, progressive, and Democratic and, in spite of the general belief, it appears that the Democrats had sufficient strength to elect Wilson had there been no third party. In 1924 the political tide was running so strongly Republican that the Republicans would have won even if LaFollette had not diverted nearly 5,000,000 votes from the Democrats.

There have been a number of elections, however, in which the two major parties were much more evenly balanced and third parties apparently wielded decisive power. Bearing in mind that it is never wise to say positively what might have been, it is nevertheless instructive to run down the hundred-year record of presidential elections and note in many the narrow margins between victory and defeat—where third parties exerted or could have exerted control.

Starting with 1844, we find that Polk, a Democrat, was elected with 49.5 per cent of the popular vote against 48.1 per cent for Clay, the Whig. In this election, the Liberty Party cast 2.3 per cent of the votes and, numerically speaking, could have swung the election to Clay.

Similarly, Van Buren's Free Soil Party in 1852, casting 10.1 per cent of the vote, could have deprived Taylor of victory by siding with the Democrat, Cass. Likewise, if Fillmore's American Party in 1856 had endorsed the Republican, Frémont, probably Buchanan would have been defeated.

Lincoln's election in 1860 is usually attributed to the split in Democratic ranks, when Southern Democrats voted for Breckenridge and Northern Democrats for Douglas. But there was also a split in the Republican Party and it is seldom observed that if the Democrats—North and South—had been united, and also the Republican factions, Lincoln might still have been elected. The Douglas vote, 29.4 per cent of the total, plus 18.1 per cent for Breckenridge, would have fallen short of a majority, while Lincoln's 39.9 per cent plus Bell's (Union Party) 12.6 per cent would have given the Republicans 52.5 per cent.

The election of 1876 is famous for the fact that Tilden, the Democratic candidate, who received the popular majority (50.9 per cent) lost the presidency to Hayes, who had only 48.0 per cent, because Congress, called upon to decide an argument over the election in one of the Southern states, decided in favor of Hayes.

Garfield in 1880 defeated Hancock with 48.3 per cent of the popular vote against his opponent's 48.2 per cent. In that election the Greenback Party, with only 3.3 per cent of the vote, could easily have kept Garfield from gaining a majority. In 1884 the Greenback Party with 1.33 per cent of the total vote could have swung the election to Blaine, who received 48.3 per cent, compared with Cleveland's 48.6 per cent.

In 1892 the People's Party—the third greatest third-party movement since the Civil War—polled 8.5 per cent of the total vote. This was more than enough to upset Cleveland's very modest 3-point margin (46.0 per cent) over Harrison (43.0 per cent), and deprive him of an electoral majority, had the People's Party decided to back Harrison instead of its own candidate.

The 1916 election would have gone differently if the Socialist (3.2 per cent) and Prohibition (1.8 per cent) vote had been combined to deprive Woodrow Wilson of his 3-point margin over Hughes.

The record is not promising for the emergence of a third party strong enough, in the first year after its organization, to draw as much as a fourth or a fifth of the total vote. Of all the third and other minor parties in the last hundred years, few have achieved numerical importance although many have exerted great influence. About five won as much as 12 to 27 per cent of the total vote in presidential races, the other seven receiving from 3 to 10 per cent. The combined list is as follows:

Third and Other Minor Parties
(in order of numerical importance)

PARTY	CANDIDATE	YEAR	PER CENT OF TOTAL VOTE
Progressive	Roosevelt	1912	27.4
American	Fillmore	1856	21.6
Democrat	Breckenridge	1860	18.1
Progressive	LaFollette	1924	16.6
Union	Bell	1860	12.6
Free Soil	Van Buren	1848	10.1
People's	Weaver	1892	8.5
Socialist	Debs	1912	6.0
Free Soil	Hale	1852	5.0
Socialist	Debs	1920	3.5
Greenback	Weaver	1880	3.3
Socialist	Debs	1904	3.0

Unsuccessful in electing their own candidates, minor-party movements have from time to time wielded great power when the two major parties were almost evenly matched, as in the five presidential elections from 1876 to 1892, when neither party received more than 52 per cent of the two-party vote.

Where do third parties recruit their greatest numbers? In general, they have the greatest appeal in states where the independent vote is relatively large and voting behavior flexible. Ordinarily that would mean, as we shall see presently, the North

Central and Western states, but much depends on the leader, issues, and groups that constitute the driving power for the third-party movement. The 1924 and 1912 campaigns suggest which states might again be involved and how large a third-party vote each might cast.

The third-party campaign in 1912 turned on issues that do not loom large today. It is therefore probably less useful than that of 1924 as background for judging the regional distribution of third-party strength in 1946, or in 1952.

One of the points at issue between Theodore Roosevelt and Taft in 1912, not present in 1948, was trade reciprocity with Canada. Today the tariff issue does not seem to be as prominent as it was in 1910–12. According to a Gallup poll at the end of 1947, 64 per cent of the Democrats and 63 per cent of the Republicans viewed favorably the international agreement reached by twenty-three nations to start downward tariff revisions in 1948. But in 1912 the tariff, combined with the conservation issue, cost Taft support in the Grain Belt, in states along the Canadian border, and in those states where forestry and logging interests and tariff-minded manufacturing industries, such as textiles, were paramount. A state-by-state measure of the relative economic importance of these interests would be an excellent index of the votes Roosevelt drew from Taft.

These interests will be found chiefly in the line of states from Maine to Washington, along the Atlantic coast from Maine to North Carolina, and down the Pacific coast from Washington through Oregon and California. Chart 11 shows that these states gave Theodore Roosevelt his greatest support.

Roosevelt in 1912 won 27 per cent of the total vote, but in Maine, New England, New York, Pennsylvania, Ohio, Michigan, Illinois, Minnesota, and all the Northwest and Pacific states he polled 25 to 50 per cent. Wisconsin, with only a 16 per cent vote for Roosevelt, was an understandable exception if it is recalled that the Bull Moose Party originated as a Western movement in behalf of LaFollette. Roosevelt won the electoral votes of two Far Western states, Washington and California, and South Dakota, Minnesota, Michigan, and Pennsylvania.

The geographic distribution of the third-party vote of 1924 is even more striking. In absolute numbers LaFollette's greatest

CHART 11

THE THEODORE ROOSEVELT THIRD-PARTY VOTE, 1912

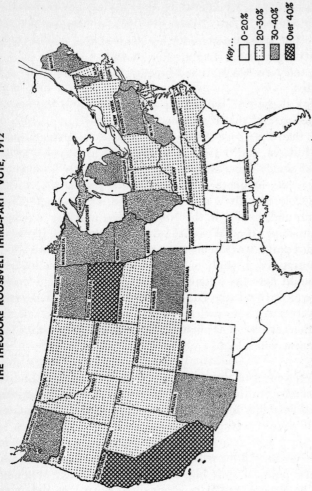

Key...

☐ 0-20%

▦ 20-30%

▨ 30-40%

▩ Over 40%

The state-by-state percentages of the presidential vote of 1912 cast for Theodore Roosevelt show greater third-party strength in the Northern and Western States than in the Southern. Note that Wisconsin held back in 1912.

strength was, of course, in the most heavily populated states. More than half his total vote was cast in the seven states: New York, Pennsylvania, Ohio, Illinois, Wisconsin, Minnesota, and California. But when we consider his share of the vote in each of the forty-eight states, LaFollette's strength was least in the Southeast and New England and greatest in the Northwest and Pacific states.

If we look at chart 12, we see a neat progression; in North and South Carolina and the Tennessee Valley states LaFollette received less than 5 per cent of the vote; in Maine, New Hampshire, Vermont, Indiana, and the rest of the South, 5 to 10 per cent; in the band of states stretching from Massachusetts to Kansas, 10 to 20 per cent; in another band of contiguous states, Iowa, Nebraska, Colorado, Utah, and Arizona, and also Oregon, 20 to 30 per cent; and, finally, in the Northwestern and Far Western states, 30 to 45 per cent. Wisconsin, the home state of LaFollette and his third party, was the only one to give him a majority.

Those interested in studying the influence of personalities in politics should note the difference between the unusually large percentage of the total vote LaFollette received in Wisconsin and the relatively small vote polled here by Theodore Roosevelt. In both elections we see LaFollette's power in his home state; in 1924 to draw votes to himself, in 1912 to divert votes from Roosevelt.

The effectiveness of the third party in 1924 may also be analyzed according to the political flexibility of the various states. By political flexibility is meant the extent to which the party vote shifts with a given change in the national vote. If there is a 10-point percentage swing in the national vote, by how many percentage points will the party vote in any state change? On the basis of the political shift between 1920 and 1936, a 10-point swing in the national ballot in either direction meant a shift in New Hampshire of only 4 points, but in North Dakota it meant a 19-point change. The indexes of flexibility for these states therefore are given as 4 and 19 in the following table.

Note how the LaFollette vote tended to correspond to this measure of political flexibility. For the states in Group I, the index of flexibility rises from 4 to 14, and in a general way the vote for LaFollette shows a corresponding increase. In the states in Group II, the index rises from 8 to 16 and the LaFollette vote

CHART 12

THE LAFOLLETTE THIRD PARTY VOTE, 1924

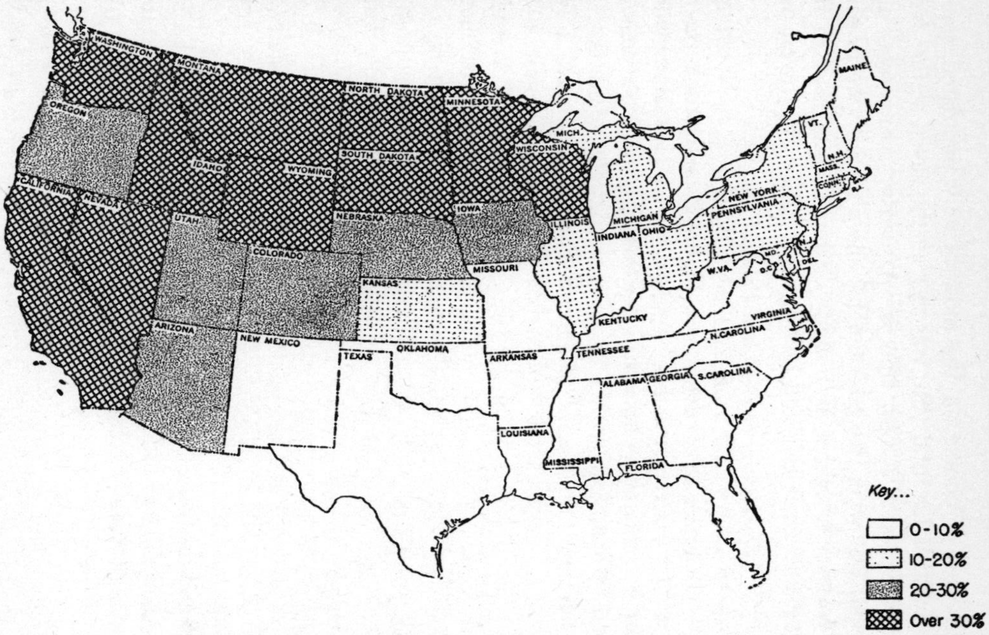

Key:...
☐ 0-10%
▧ 10-20%
▨ 20-30%
▩ Over 30%

The state-by-state percentages and the presidential vote for LaFollette in 1924 show a Northwestern progression. Third-party strength was greatest in the Northern and Far Western states and least in the Tennessee Valley states of the South.

from 15 to 36 per cent. In the third group, the index rises from 11 to 19 and the LaFollette votes from 32 to 45 per cent.

A new third party may also find its support greatest in the Northwestern states having the greatest political flexibility, and least in the relatively stable states—especially if the issues of 1924 represent a reasonable parallel.

Third-Party Strength and Political Flexibility

STATE	INDEX OF FLEXI- BILITY	% OF VOTE FOR LA- FOLLETTE	STATE	INDEX OF FLEXI- BILITY	% OF VOTE FOR LA- FOLLETTE
Group I			Group II		
New Hampshire	4	6	Kansas	8	15
Maine	5	6	Colorado	10	20
Delaware	5	6	Nebraska	10	23
Indiana	6	6	Arizona	11	23
Maryland	7	13	Utah	11	21
Vermont	8	6	Iowa	11	28
Ohio	8	15	Oregon	13	25
Rhode Island	9	4	California	16	33
Connecticut	9	11	Washington	16	36
Massachusetts	10	13	Group III		
New York	11	14	Wyoming	11	32
Pennsylvania	11	14	Idaho	12	37
New Jersey	12	10	South Dakota	12	37
Illinois	12	18	Nevada	13	36
Michigan	14	11	Montana	14	38
			Minnesota	17	41
			Wisconsin	19	54
			North Dakota	19	45

NOTE: In two thirds of the sixteen Southern states not included in these groups, the LaFollette third party received 4 to 8 per cent, with a low of 1.2 per cent in South Carolina and a high of 9.5 per cent in Arkansas.

The extent to which a third party can affect election results in any state depends on the relative strength of the two major parties. In 1924, LaFollette's Progressives drew votes chiefly from the Democratic ranks, but this didn't affect the results of the election. On the other hand, had a third party been in the field in 1944, the outcome might have been altogether different. With the nation voting only 54 per cent Democratic, a third party need have drawn only 3 per cent of the votes from the Democratic or Republican camp to shift the electoral balance in such states as New York, Pennsylvania, New Jersey, Missouri, Minnesota, Indiana, Illinois, Connecticut, Ohio, Michigan, Massachusetts, Indiana, Iowa, New Hampshire, Oregon, Wisconsin, and Wyoming. All these went Democratic or Republican in 1944 by less than a 3 per cent margin. It is in such situations that third-party movements have the greatest opportunity for wielding their power so effectively that they may actually decide the outcome of a national election.

The boldest crystal-gazer, if wise, will constantly bear in mind that predicting elections in the midst of a political whirlpool like that of early 1948 is obviously hazardous. Ordinarily the range of possibilities in a two-party battle is fairly narrow even before the candidates are chosen. The appearance of a third party greatly complicates the difficulties of forecasting, even after the three candidates are chosen.

By the beginning of 1948, possible presidential candidates included the incumbent, popular generals, aspiring governors with good records in New York and California, an ex-governor of Minnesota, a former vice president (heading a third-party movement), and many obviously pawing "dark horses." The possible combinations and permutations consequently made long-range statistical prediction practically meaningless unless confined within a specified set of assumptions.

After the Republican and Democratic candidates are chosen, the prediction of elections with a third party in the field would require answering two questions. How would the Republicans and Democrats fare, state by state, if they had the field to themselves? How many votes will the third-party candidate draw from the major parties? The basic material for these analyses is presented in the succeeding chapters, particularly in Chapter 11, which contains normal schedules of electoral votes by states for various combinations of Republican-Democratic strength, together with some indication of what third-party and other influences could do in given situations.

Chapter 8:

Political Patterns

      The general pattern of two-party voting behavior in presidential years was sketched in the preceding chapter. This pattern, showing two Democratic peaks, 1912 and 1936, and two bottoms, 1904 and 1924, is of course a composite of the voting behavior of the forty-eight states. Which states contribute most to the shaping of that national pattern? In which is the national pattern most clearly reflected? Are there sectional similarities, East, West, North, and South? Are there similarities within each of these regions? Are some states more politically stable than others? Do some of the states ever go against the national trend? If so, why?

      Answers to these and many other questions are contained in the panorama of the political behavior of each state over a period of forty-eight years, in charts 13 to 18.

      Were I to show the numerical votes state by state and party by party for forty-eight years covering thirteen presidential elections, I should overwhelm the reader with a mass of unappetizing

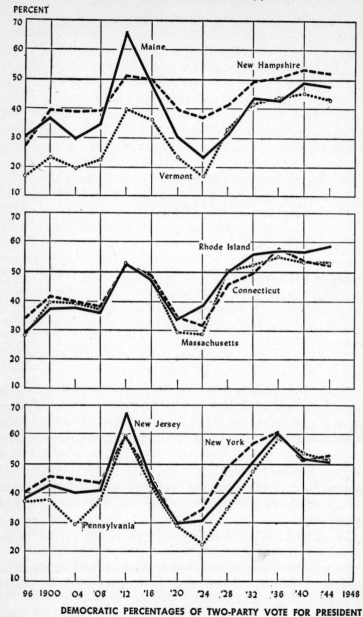

POLITICAL PATTERN IN THE NORTHEAST (1)

PERCENT

Maine

New Hampshire

Vermont

Rhode Island

Connecticut

Massachusetts

New Jersey

New York

Pennsylvania

96 1900 04 '08 '12 '16 '20 '24 '28 '32 '36 '40 '44 1948

DEMOCRATIC PERCENTAGES OF TWO-PARTY VOTE FOR PRESIDENT

CHART 13

figures. There is a real pitfall in mere numbers not always avoided
by commentators and politicians who seem to prefer to speak in
terms of absolute number of votes cast and the number of votes
by which one candidate leads another. Since the population of
the nation or a given state or locality has been constantly increasing, the total ballots cast today may have no more significance than a smaller number ten or twenty years ago; in fact,
may be misleading. I have, therefore, converted the figures into
simple two-party percentages charted so that their main features
can be grasped quickly.

Keeping the national pattern in mind, particularly the depths
to which Democratic fortunes sank in 1904 and 1924 and the
heights reached in 1912 and 1936, let us make the round of the
states and survey the political records shown on pages 79–89.
What should we look for as we make our political tour? First we
observe that the states are arranged in three major groups;
eighteen Northeastern and North Central states forming the
first; eighteen Western states the second; and twelve Southern
the third. The first two have been further subdivided into groups
of three on the basis of contiguity, each constituting a geographic
unit.

Other features that attract our attention are: the unique pattern of the South in contrast with the pattern common to the
Northern and Western states; the much wider swings in the political tides in the Western states where readiness to shift from
one party to another is most noticeable; the persistence of Democratic predominance in some states and Republican in others,
irrespective of national issues; the tendency for some states to
become more and more Democratic, for others to become more
and more Republican; and the peculiarities or dissimilarities in
certain state patterns that suggest the existence and effect of
special issues.

The central fact that strikes our eye in the survey is the
prevalence of a common pattern in the two groups of states outside the South. This degree of uniformity is of much value to the
student of politics and the would-be prognosticator. Of course
there are differences as well as similarities in voting behavior, but
the differences take on even greater significance against the background of uniformity in the behavior of the nation. Where there
are discrepancies, there must be causes, and the mere noting of

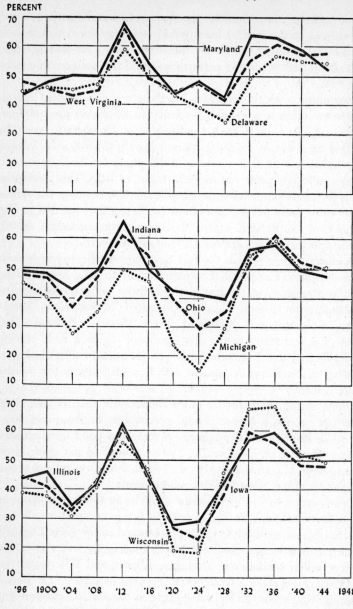

POLITICAL PATTERN IN THE NORTHEAST (2)

PERCENT

Maryland

West Virginia

Delaware

Indiana

Ohio

Michigan

Illinois

Iowa

Wisconsin

'96 1900 '04 '08 '12 '16 '20 '24 '28 '32 '36 '40 '44 1948

DEMOCRATIC PERCENTAGES OF TWO-PARTY VOTE FOR PRESIDENT

CHART 14

these discrepancies stimulates the student to search for the causes.

Political students who have wondered whether voters in old Maine and younger California, industrial New York and agricultural Iowa, follow similar patterns will find the answers in charts 13 to 18.

Beginning with the eighteen Northeastern and North Central states, we observe a general tendency to adhere to the national cycle; all climbed from a relatively low Democratic vote in 1900–4 to peaks in 1912–16, dipped low in 1920–4, and swung high again in 1932–6. Four states in this group reached the second Democratic low point not in 1920–4, but in 1928. This deviation from the more common experience immediately raises the question: were there particular reasons in these states for the strong opposition to Alfred E. Smith, the Democratic candidate, or for the support given his opponent, Herbert Hoover?

A closer glance reveals the fact that these cyclical swings vary in magnitude. The smallest variation prior to 1932 appeared in the Northeastern states forming the three geographical units: Massachusetts, Rhode Island, Connecticut; Maine, New Hampshire, Vermont; and Maryland, West Virginia, Indiana. The North Central states in this first group of eighteen have shown wider fluctuations between the two major parties, with Michigan leading in flexibility, in contrast with less flexibility in the Northeastern states.

Some states are normally more Democratic than others; they fluctuate around a higher pivotal percentage. For example, Vermont—a Republican stronghold—pivots on a point on the chart about 30 per cent Democratic; Maine around 35 per cent; New Hampshire, Massachusetts, Rhode Island, and Connecticut about 40 per cent; and West Virginia, 45 per cent.

Some states in this group show a tendency to become increasingly Democratic. Whether or not this is a permanent trend, it is worth observing that it is quite pronounced in the New England states, a little less markedly in Maine than in the other five. We find a similar tendency in Michigan, Illinois, and Wisconsin.

Other states show a tendency to become increasingly Republican, or what comes to the same thing in our charts, less and less Democratic. We see this in the record for Delaware and Indiana.

A general view of the eighteen Midwestern and Far Western states, contained in the second section of this panorama, reveals

POLITICAL PATTERN IN THE WEST (1)

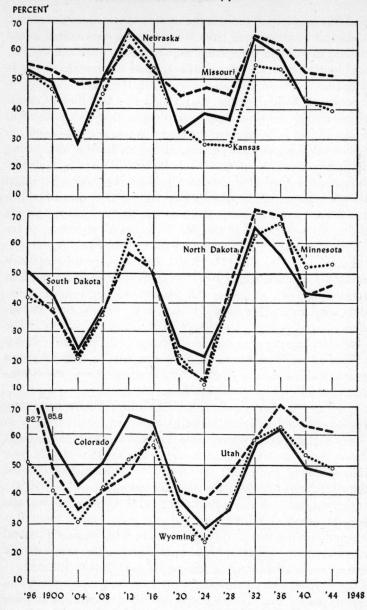

DEMOCRATIC PERCENTAGES OF TWO-PARTY VOTE FOR PRESIDENT

CHART 15

patterns similar to those of the Eastern and North Central states. But in this area we find greater extremes in the political swings and several striking abnormalities.

Note, for example, within what a narrow range the curve for Missouri fluctuates and compare it with the broader swings for Minnesota, North Dakota, and California. We find again the rising trends in Democratic strength first observed in the New England states; this time in the opposite corner of the country— Idaho, Washington, and Oregon. But seven Northwestern states, Utah, Wyoming, North and South Dakota, Minnesota, Colorado, and Kansas, suggest a downward trend. The states in which Democratic strength reached a low point in 1928 instead of 1920 and 1924 are contiguous to the Southern region—Missouri, Oklahoma, Arizona, and New Mexico.

One abnormality in political behavior in this area occurred in the 1912 election, when the Republican organizations of South Dakota and California gave their entire support to Theodore Roosevelt. For that reason the Democratic percentages of the two-party vote (Democratic and Republican) in 1912 are not shown in the patterns for these two states.

In 1896 another abnormality shows up in the political patterns of Colorado, Nevada, Idaho, and Montana—all silver-mining states. The central plank in the Democratic platform, the monetization of silver, so appealed to these states that they gave Bryan more than 70 per cent of their two-party vote, as indicated by the figures entered on charts 15 and 16.

We find a third abnormality in the 1916 elections in Montana, Idaho, Utah, and Wyoming. The patterns for these states show Democratic peaks in 1916 instead of 1912. This obviously reflects the added support given the international policies of the Wilson administration and possibly the return of Democrats who had gone Progressive in 1912.

Another observation should be made with respect to states reaching their New Deal peaks in 1936. Not all gave the Democrats a larger percentage of their votes in 1936 than 1932. In the Eastern and North Central states the 1936 percentages were generally greater than in 1932, but Maine, Maryland, and more noticeably Iowa deviated from this general pattern in the Eastern and North Central regions. In the Western group the departure from the general trend in 1936 was quite pronounced in Kansas,

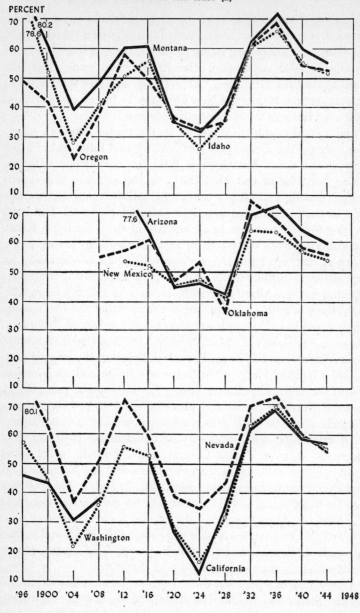

POLITICAL PATTERN IN THE WEST (2)

DEMOCRATIC PERCENTAGES OF TWO-PARTY VOTE FOR PRESIDENT

CHART 16

Nebraska, Missouri, Oklahoma, North Dakota, and South Dakota. To some extent this deviation seems to have been a reaction from the sharp and temporary swing to the Democratic Party induced by the 1929–32 depression. The Republicans made their first gains against the New Deal tide in this area. From this center of defection opposition to the New Deal can be traced eastward and westward through the elections of 1940 and 1944.

Quite another story is recorded by the twelve Southern states. Not only do the Democrats here usually cast more than 50 per cent of the votes, but there is little correspondence with the voting behavior of the other thirty-six states. South Carolina is unique, having cast 95 per cent of its ballots on the Democratic side in each of the last seven presidential elections. The most striking feature common to all but two of these Southern states, but differing from the trend for most of the other states, is the sharp reduction in the Democratic vote in 1928—obviously an expression of anti-Catholic and in part an anti-wet sentiment directed against Alfred E. Smith. In view of this Southern attitude, there is added significance to the fact that the Democratic percentages in 1928 went lower than in 1924 in Kansas, Nebraska, Missouri, Oklahoma, Arizona, New Mexico, Maryland, Delaware, West Virginia, and Indiana. Here, too, I suspect the play of anti-Catholic feeling. The specific factor of religion and its power to distort the political patterns, raising the Democratic percentages in some Northern states and lowering them below the Mason-Dixon line, will be dealt with in greater detail in the next chapter.

Other striking differences may be noted in the 1940 and 1944 elections. Western, North Central, and Mountain states show greater Democratic losses than elsewhere, but the New England and Pacific coast states remained practically stable. The explanation for this discrepancy is the tendency for the Northeastern and Far Western states to support the administration in time of war, while the Central states remain somewhat isolationist and so less sympathetic to the administration in power. This matter, too, is dealt with in greater detail in the next chapter.

One would imagine that the growth of industrialization in the United States and the westward shift of our population during the years covered by this record would produce differences in *normal* political trends, with Democratic fortunes rising gradually in some states and declining in others. I have already pointed to

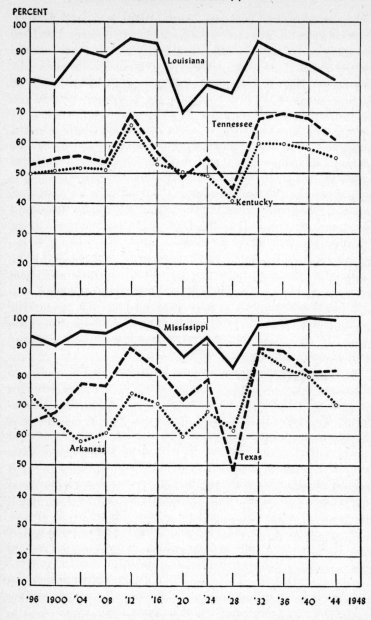

POLITICAL PATTERN IN THE SOUTH (1)

PERCENT

Louisiana

Tennessee

Kentucky

Mississippi

Arkansas

Texas

'96 1900 '04 '08 '12 '16 '20 '24 '28 '32 '36 '40 '44 1948

DEMOCRATIC PERCENTAGES OF TWO-PARTY VOTE FOR PRESIDENT

CHART 17

the upward tendency in Democratic strength in New England, some Eastern, North Central (Michigan, Illinois, Wisconsin, Minnesota, North and South Dakota), and Far Western states. But in viewing the long-time results from 1896–1900 to 1936–44, we must recognize the special economic and political problems that prevailed at the beginning and end of this period—the basis of our comparisons—in order to avoid wrong impressions. For example, in New England the silver issue of the 1890's tended to militate against the Democrats, while in 1940 and 1944 international difficulties and world war definitely strengthened their position. It is probably such major factors, plus the wide cyclical swings of the political pendulum, that obscure an underlying upward Democratic trend in presidential voting corresponding to the trend we observed in the Democratic percentage of House membership. The fifty-year record of rural and urban voting, if examined state by state, would show even more marked differences than the regional voting behavior, with pronounced accessions of voters to the Democratic Party in urban centers.

Much of what follows in subsequent chapters is based on these political records for the forty-eight states, and if the reader will study the charts carefully, his way through the facts may be less tedious and more sure-footed.

At the risk of oversimplification, I would offer the reader two keys as aids toward a general appreciation of what this panorama of political patterns contains. One is similarity, the other dissimilarity. The general similarities, particularly in voting habits in Northern and Western states, are traceable to the common, universal impact of the business depressions of 1932 and 1920; possibly also to the delayed effect of the 1908 depression and the reform movements producing the Progressive Party and Woodrow Wilson's election in 1912. The dissimilarities are traceable to the issues that affect groups and regions differently. In the following pages are discussed in some detail the silver issue in 1896 and 1904, the two wars and opposition to them among some of our nationality groups in 1916, 1940, and 1944, and the religious bias evident in 1928. These are the outstanding issues that produced the most striking regional differences in voting behavior in the thirteen presidential elections since 1896.

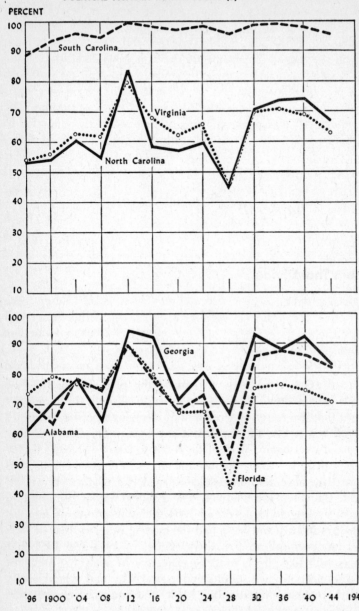

POLITICAL PATTERN IN THE SOUTH (2)

PERCENT

South Carolina

Virginia

North Carolina

Georgia

Alabama

Florida

'96 1900 '04 '08 '12 '16 '20 '24 '28 32 '36 '40 '44 1948

DEMOCRATIC PERCENTAGES OF TWO-PARTY VOTE FOR PRESIDENT

CHART 18

Chapter 9:

Issues That Divide

One needs only to look at the platforms of the two major parties down through the years to observe the numerous issues that are raised in presidential elections in order to attract voters. Some, like the tariff and anti-monopoly planks, appear over and over again. Most of them cut in many directions and it is difficult to see their separate influences in election results. But those that have left unmistakable evidence of their power to divide the voters are relatively few. Political battles centering on silver versus gold in 1896 and 1904, isolationism versus internationalism in 1916 and 1940, and the evident religious bias in 1928 may not be duplicated in the elections of 1948 and 1952, but others with like effects must be expected. In analyzing and predicting elections, we should understand why and where voters depart from their usual voting habits and find some quantitative measure of response to major controversial issues. And, particularly, we must know whether prewar isolationism, which added to Republican strength in the Central states in 1940 and still lingered as a factor in 1944, is likely to influence citizens in 1948 and 1952.

Silver versus Gold

The great silver issue at the turn of the century affected voters according to the expected effect on their pocketbooks. It came at the end of a twenty-year decline in prices following the inflation after the Civil War. Low agricultural prices in the depression of 1890, together with prolonged unemployment in the industrial centers, formed part of the economic background that led the Democratic Party in 1896 to accept Bryan as its candidate and promise to put silver into circulation as a legal-money metal at the ratio of sixteen ounces to one of gold. Because the monetization of silver was expected to raise agricultural prices, this issue is usually considered to have drawn a political line between the farming and industrial areas. The three elections of 1896, 1900, and 1904, however, show that actually it was more a battle between the Western states with silver-mining interests and the Eastern states with banking and international interests. The silver-producing states naturally favored a higher price and expanded market for their product. The Eastern states, with accumulated wealth and local and state bonded indebtedness, didn't want the gold standard diluted with silver and the purchasing power of their securities and incomes endangered by inflated prices.

The Easterners believed that the gold standard should not be tinkered with, certainly not without international agreement. They believed in the economic law of the textbooks that in a bi-metal standard the cheaper, silver, drives the dearer, gold, from circulation; they also believed quite realistically that rising prices cut the purchasing power of the population that lives on salaries, interest, dividends, and other types of fixed or stable incomes.

These opposing economic points of view were most clearly reflected in the 1896 and 1904 campaigns. In noting the behavior of the Western and Eastern states in these two elections, bear in mind that the silver-gold issue dominated the 1896 campaign; that in 1900, while Bryan was again the Democratic candidate, the silver issue had already been resolved by Congress in favor

of gold; and that in 1904, when the silver issue was revived by a
Western group in the Democratic Party, the Democratic candidate (Alton B. Parker), an Easterner, openly announced his
opposition to diluting the gold standard. This cost him the support of Bryan and many of Bryan's followers and explains why
the states that favored the Great Commoner in 1896 voted against
Parker in 1904.

Selecting only those states that voted 5 percentage points more
Democratic in 1896 than in 1900, we find that the following
fourteen apparently favored the monetization of silver. Of the
seven states with substantially larger Democratic percentages—
10 to 34 per cent—in 1896 than in 1900, practically all produced
some silver.

*States with Larger Democratic Votes in 1896 than
in 1900:*

(PERCENTAGE POINTS)

Minnesota	+5	Wyoming	+10
Kansas	+5	Washington	+13
Alabama	+6	Nevada	+18
Oregon	+7	Montana	+21
North Dakota	+8	Idaho	+26
South Dakota	+8	Colorado	+29
Arkansas	+8	Utah	+34

At the other extreme were ten states that voted less Democratic
in 1896 than in 1900. Eight were in the Northeastern section,
which had then and still has more than average per capita wealth,
savings, industrial, banking, and commercial assets.

*States with a Smaller Democratic Vote in 1896 than
in 1900:*

(PERCENTAGE POINTS)

Maine	− 6	Rhode Island	−9
New Hampshire	−12	New York	−5
Vermont	− 7	New Jersey	−5
Massachusetts	−12	Georgia	−9
Connecticut	− 8	Florida	−6

The same regional economic alignment was evident in the 1904
election. The Democratic Party was handicapped by the stronger
personality of the Republican candidate, Theodore Roosevelt; by
Alton B. Parker's acceptance of the Republican stand on the

silver-gold issue; and by Bryan's consequent opposition to Parker. The foregoing states that in 1896 had given Bryan more than the usual Democratic support shifted violently to Roosevelt. The Democratic candidate received 13 to 24 percentage points less in the Northwestern states than Bryan did in 1900, while in the New England and Middle Atlantic regions the Democrats practically held their ground with an average loss of only two points.

Isolationism versus Internationalism

Economic interests sway voters in all elections, but issues that set off nationality groups from each other crop up only now and then. The most recent manifestation occurred in the elections of 1940 and 1944 when German-American citizens voted as on two other, broadly similar occasions. In 1916, when we were helping but not yet participating in World War I, the isolationist voters, including some German-Americans chiefly in the Middle West and Northwest, deserted Wilson at a greater rate than those in the international-minded Eastern and Far Western states. To a more marked degree, in 1940, when we were helping but not yet actually fighting in World War II, the German-Americans—and in some communities the Italian-Americans—shifted quite noticeably to Willkie.

The third episode (not generally known) is the defection of German-Americans who, in cities like New York, St. Louis, and Milwaukee, had voted strongly for Cleveland in 1884, but contributed to his defeat in 1888. This reversal is associated with what is known as the Samoa incident. Germany, the United States, and Great Britain were then bound by a tripartite agreement with regard to governing the Pacific island of Samoa. Germany attempted to break the agreement and set up its own ruler. Strained relations, with battleships gathered near Samoa and actual firing of shots while the election campaign was in progress, turned German-American votes away from Cleveland. Thus three roughly identical cases, involving the same nationality ties, resulted in similar reactions at the polls.

In my study *Ballot Behavior,* published shortly after the 1940 conventions, the possibility of a sag in the Democratic vote in the Middle states (in view of the 1916 results) was indicated. The sag actually developed in such pronounced form as to suggest a statistical journey into 1940 isolationism.

With the country as a whole voting 55 per cent Democratic in 1940, my statistical studies had indicated that the Democrats in Maine would normally poll 39 per cent of the vote; actually they obtained 49 per cent, or 10 points above normal. Massachusetts, which should have given 48 per cent to the Democrats, gave 53 per cent, or 5 points above normal. Missouri should have voted 57 per cent Democratic, but fell short by 5 points. Nebraska fell by 10 points, but in California and Washington the Democrats exceeded normal by 3 points. The Democratic sag is clearly revealed in a block of Central states extending from North Dakota to Texas, shown below together with the percentage points by which they departed from normal in 1940.

	PERCENTAGE POINTS
North Dakota	−12
Nebraska	−10
Colorado	− 6
South Dakota	− 5
Kansas	−16
Oklahoma	− 5
Texas	− 3

Naturally I was interested in the reason for this phenomenon. During the campaign there was a good deal of speculation about the isolationist vote, its magnitude, and in which population groups it would appear. There was particular concern about communities with citizens of German or Italian descent. The German-language press played up the Republican candidate as *one of us*, just as Smith in 1928 was considered to be the favorite among Catholics. Citizens of German origin were subjected to much anti-administration and pro-German propaganda, and many probably still remembered the harsh treatment they had received during the first World War.

The frank appeal to such groups is illustrated by the following advertisement addressed to Americans of German origin:

NOTICE—AMERICANS OF GERMAN ORIGIN
The election which takes place on Nov. 5th of this year is one of the most important in the history of the United States.

One President of the United States, One Governor of the State of Illinois, and other state, county and local officers are to be chosen.

The Republican ticket presents for the office of President, an American whose father, mother and grandparents, and whose in-laws were born in Germany—Wendell L. Willkie—a German-American whose rise is due directly to his own efforts.

At the head of the ticket for the State of Illinois, for the office of Governor, is another German-American whose parents were German—Dwight H. Green. These candidates have come to the front in real American style. They are an example of what can be done by anyone who will make the sacrifice. We ask you to vote for these candidates, not because of their origin, but because they have proved themselves loyal Americans.

On the Republican ticket, national, state and local, are many German-Americans who are candidates for various offices. You therefore have an opportunity of voting for German-Americans, which opportunity you have so often demanded. Vote right. Vote for the entire Republican ticket, from top to bottom, from President to the last candidate for Judge in the City of Chicago. [*Daily Times*, Chicago, October 15, 1940, p. 34. Translation of an anonymous advertisement in *Sontagpost*, Chicago, October 13, 1940.]

The first test in ascertaining the strength of the isolationist vote was very simple. I chose as the area of my experiment the entire western tier of Minnesota counties bordering North Dakota, and noted that the Democratic vote here dropped 3 to 22 percentage points between 1936 and 1940. These losses were in direct proportion to the number of German-Americans in the counties. Where only 3 per cent of the population was of German parentage, the Democrats lost 3 percentage points to Willkie, but in counties where, say, 15 to 20 per cent were of German origin, the vote shifted approximately 15 to 20 points to Willkie.

This experiment gave such striking results that it impelled further research. I applied my technique to the southern and central tiers of Minnesota counties, again finding striking corroboration of the relationship between the proportion of German-Americans and Republican gains.

To make doubly sure, I next cross-sectioned Iowa counties and found the same correspondence. Along the southern tier Republican gains were small and so was the German strain in the population. In some of the northern counties, where the Republicans made as much headway as in southern Minnesota, the German element was more predominant.

To make trebly sure, I investigated the election results in Wisconsin and Nebraska. There, too, the same statistical correspondence showed up.

Could it be that I was dealing with certain characteristics of the Middle West, not necessarily related to particular ties of nationality? I therefore next investigated the political shift in the East. New York State, I assumed, certainly would be a good test. Here I found two different situations. In up-state counties along the St. Lawrence River and Lake Ontario, there were relatively few Germans and a fair number of Canadians of English ancestry. Where Germans constituted less than 5 per cent of the total population, the Democrats were stronger in 1940 than in 1936; but in counties having more than 5 per cent Germans, the Democrats lost ground.

In the down-state metropolitan counties I first encountered what seemed like real evidence that I was entirely on the wrong statistical track. Here the correspondence between Democratic losses and German population percentages was not nearly so close as in other areas. For example, Richmond County, with less than 10 per cent German stock, showed a 16-point Democratic loss; Queens, with 17 per cent German population, showed much the same results. The reason for this discrepancy, however, was not difficult to discover. It will be recalled that during the 1940 campaign there was a great deal of concern over the Italian voters who resented the President's "Stab-in-the-Back" speech after Italy entered the war. While Richmond County has fewer Germans than Queens, it contains relatively more Italians. I found, therefore, that the proportion of these two population elements taken together yielded the typical close correspondence with Democratic losses.

No more statistically convincing proof than this was needed, yet it seemed desirable to try one or two more tests. I turned back to North Dakota, reasoning that an examination of its voting behavior should yield the same conclusions as did its neighboring state, Minnesota. I lined up the Democratic losses for groups of North Dakota counties with the corresponding German population data and received an even greater statistical jolt than when I had first examined the New York City data. I found that in many counties a veritable political revolution had taken place. Those that had voted 65 to 75 per cent Democratic in 1932 and

1936 had swung in the opposite direction so violently as to give the Republicans an actual majority in 1940. The Democrats in 1936 won 69 per cent of the votes but dropped to 44 per cent in 1940, twice the shift indicated by the usual flexibility of the state. In individual counties the swing was even greater. But the fact that shocked me and nearly killed my faith in statistical evidence was the insignificance of the German-American population in the counties where the Republicans had gained so greatly!

Fortunately, before discarding the whole experiment, I took one more look at the census population statistics on North Dakota and observed a peculiar fact. In the counties where the dramatic political shifts occurred in 1940, instead of our expected German group the census table listed a correspondingly large proportion of the population as Russian. Obviously the statistical thing to do was to combine the Russian and German percentages, even though for my study it didn't seem to make sense. What did I find? The same close correspondence between population groups and political shifts as in the other tests. Where Germans and Russians constituted 10 to 20 per cent of the population, the vote shifted about 20 percentage points; those 50 to 70 per cent German and Russian shifted 40 to 50 points.

But why should Russian and German groups in North Dakota respond to the Republican campaign in the same way? No line of reasoning seemed to give an answer. In desperation I button-holed a friend who knows his North Dakota and asked him about those Russians. "They are not Russians," he said. "They are Germans. Their schools are German; their newspapers are German. They are descended from the Germans who migrated first to Russia and later to the United States. That is why the census lists them as Russian." My faith in statistics was restored.

One further experiment is worth mentioning. In predominantly Democratic Texas a few counties had gone Republican in 1940. My curiosity was aroused. On investigation I found that the area contained another cultural island, with a large portion of the population of German stock. Washington, Comal, Fayette, Lee, Austin, and Guadalupe counties, voting 70 to 80 per cent Democratic in 1936, swung 25 to 48 points toward the Republican side. In neighboring counties the shift was only 3 to 10 points. Explanation of this phenomenon is again found in the German population. Counties with only 3 to 10 per cent Germans shifted 3 to 10 points; those with 15 to 20 per cent, 24 to 48 points, right into the Republican column.

This cultural island assumes real significance in national politics for it may be credited with having elected the junior Senator from Texas. Campaigning in 1941 against a supporter of the Roosevelt administration, he received considerable support in predominantly German counties. His margin of victory was so narrow— only 1,200 votes—that a shift of only 600 votes in three rural counties with large proportions of German population would have thrown the election to the pro-Roosevelt candidate.

A large portion of the voters who in 1940 deserted Roosevelt for Willkie remained on the Republican side in 1944. The same may be said of the 1940 Republicans who in that year gave Roosevelt their vote. This is evident in the following tabulation showing to what extent the Eastern and Western states shifted to Roosevelt in 1940 and 1944, and the Central states to the Republicans. The few exceptions are Nevada, New Mexico, Arizona, Wyoming, Montana, and Maryland, where the 1944 Democratic vote was

Percentage Points by which Eastern, Central, and Western States Voted More or Less Democratic than Normal [1] in 1940 and 1944

EASTERN STATES			CENTRAL STATES		
	1940	*1944*		*1940*	*1944*
Maine	+10.3	+9.6	Arizona	− 1.1	− 4.9
Vermont	+ 7.9	+6.6	Minnesota	− 1.3	+ 1.5
Rhode Island	+ 5.7	+8.4	Idaho	− 1.5	− 2.9
New Hampshire	+ 5.6	+5.0	New Mexico	− 1.6	− 3.9
Massachusetts	+ 5.4	+5.9	Ohio	− 1.5	− 2.9
Pennsylvania	+ 3.9	+3.0	Montana	− 1.8	− 5.1
Connecticut	+ 2.6	+2.6	Wisconsin	− 2.7	− 3.5
Delaware	+ 2.6	+3.0	Texas	− 3.5	− 2.8
Illinois	+ .6	+2.3	Missouri	− 4.6	− 4.9
Michigan	+ 1.4	+3.6	Oklahoma	− 4.8	− 6.2
Maryland	+ .8	−5.5	South Dakota	− 4.5	− 4.2
New York	+ .5	+2.5	Indiana	− 4.1	− 5.6
Iowa	+ .3	+1.4	Oregon	− 5.1	− 5.3
WESTERN STATES			Kansas	− 5.7	− 7.5
Wyoming	+ .2	−2.8	Colorado	− 5.5	− 6.5
Utah	+ .8	+ .2	North Dakota	−12.3	− 7.0
Washington	+2.7	+3.0	Nevada	− 2.8	− 7.1
California	+3.4	+3.7	Nebraska	− 9.9	−10.0

[1] *Normal* as shown in App. table 8, when the national Democratic percentage is 54 per cent (as in 1944) and 55 per cent (as in 1940).

somewhat smaller than in 1940, and Rhode Island, New York, Michigan, Minnesota, and North Dakota, where it was somewhat larger.

Religious Bias

Religion is sometimes a more powerful factor in distorting normal political behavior than economic interests, or even issues of war and peace. The 1928 experience, when anti-Catholic feeling was strong enough to turn several traditionally Democratic states to the Republican candidate, will color the judgment of politicians for a long time to come. Sometimes it may color their judgment too strongly, as I suspect was the case in 1940, when Democratic leaders rated James Farley's chances as presidential candidate very low because he was a Catholic. They probably failed to consider that in 1928, when the country was 41 per cent Democratic, the net effect of the anti-Smith campaign was to reduce the Democratic electoral total in the South by about 70 votes (as shown in Chapter 11). Had the country then been more evenly divided—say, 55 per cent Democratic and 45 per cent Republican in 1940—the Democratic losses in the South would have been offset by gains in other states. A political campaign in 1940 similar to that of 1928 might have left the national balance unchanged at about 55 per cent Democratic and we would have demonstrated, by electing a Catholic to the presidency, that in our national politics we can rise above religious prejudice.

On the basis of normal patterns in voting behavior in the various states we can trace the abnormal influence of religion. When the nation in 1928 gave 41 per cent of its votes to the Democrats, Kentucky, for example, should have given them 52 per cent instead of 41, a defection of 11 points. The vote in Massachusetts should have been 35 per cent Democratic instead of 50.0 per cent, an excess of 15 points. We cannot say precisely to what degree the anti-Catholic bias caused the defection in Kentucky nor the exact contribution of the large Catholic element to the Democratic surplus in Massachusetts, since we have no exact measures of religious bias. Furthermore there was some opposition to Al Smith because he favored repeal of prohibition.

Many voters undoubtedly objected to him on both counts, religion and prohibition.

That the religious issue was dominant is demonstrated conclusively, apart from our general knowledge of the 1928 election, in the incontrovertible evidence seen in the close correspondence between state-by-state discrepancies in the 1928 vote and the proportion of Catholics, as measured by church membership.

In 1926 Catholics constituted less than 10 per cent of church membership in ten states: Florida, Georgia, South Carolina, North Carolina, Virginia, Alabama, Mississippi, Arkansas, Oklahoma, and Utah. In all but two of these the Democratic vote fell 11 to 27 per cent short of normal in 1920. At the other extreme, in all but four of the eighteen states where Catholics constituted more than 40 per cent of the total church membership the Democratic vote that year was greater than normal.

The nature of the relationship between church membership and the vote for Al Smith in 1928 can be seen more clearly by examining data for contiguous states. Groups of states that form geographic units, that are economically and culturally interrelated, may be expected to show consistent responses to major economic and political issues. One such group includes North Carolina, Virginia, West Virginia, Kentucky, Illinois, Indiana, Michigan, Ohio, Pennsylvania, New York, New Jersey, Connecticut, and Massachusetts. The proportion of Catholics in the total population of church members and the corresponding shortage or excess in the 1928 Democratic vote is shown in the next table.

We may note that the range in Catholic church membership here varies from 3 to 65 per cent, a spread of 62 points, while the range in percentages of the Democratic votes varies from minus 20 to plus 15, or 35 points. From this tabulation we may draw the generalization that state A, with 20 per cent more Catholics in its church membership than state B, gave Smith an additional 10 per cent of its total vote. Or, conversely, state C, with 20 per cent more Protestants than state D, deprived Smith of 10 per cent of its total vote.

This conclusion is corroborated by similar comparisons for other groups of contiguous states, such as Texas, Louisiana, Arizona, New Mexico; Oregon, Washington, Nevada, and California; and Idaho, Iowa, Wyoming, and South Dakota.

Why did states with an equal proportion of Roman Catholics—

for example, 24 per cent in Texas and Oregon—behave quite differently at the polls in 1928; the one dropping 33 points, the other only 5. This may indicate merely that membership in the Catholic Church in itself is an inadequate measure of religious bias in politics, or that economic factors also were responsible for

Roman Catholic Church Membership and the 1928
Democratic Presidential Vote
(14 selected states)

STATE	CATHOLIC PER CENT CHURCH MEMBERSHIP	PER CENT DEPARTURE OF 1928 DEMO. VOTE FROM NORMAL [1]
Virginia	3	−20
North Carolina	4	−17
West Virginia	13	− 9
Kentucky	17	−11
Indiana	23	− 8
Ohio	34	0
Illinois	40	+ 7
Pennsylvania	41	+ 5
New York	46	+ 9
Michigan	47	+ 4
New Jersey	53	+10
Vermont	55	+10
Connecticut	58	+10
Massachusetts	65	+15
Range:	62	35

(Virginia-Massachusetts)

[1] *Normal* is the Democratic percentage for each state based on the 1924 and 1932 election results and corresponds to a national Democratic vote of 41 per cent.

the 1928 election results. For example, in areas where there was not only a large Catholic population but also a keen interest in the repeal of prohibition (promised by Smith), the Democratic vote naturally would have been greater than where the religious factor alone existed. Even without additional refinements in this analysis, the general response of the different states when religious bias entered the 1928 campaign is clear.

These statistical analyses add to our general knowledge the possibility that Democratic losses in Southern states can be offset by Democratic gains in the North, and that in a year when the

Roman Catholic Church Membership and the 1928
Democratic Presidential Vote
(4 selected groups of states)

STATE GROUP	CATHOLIC PERCENTAGE	PER CENT DE- PARTURE OF 1928 DEMOCRATIC VOTE FROM NORMAL [1]
Group I:		
Alabama	3	−23
Florida	7	−27
Oklahoma	8	−23
Tennessee	25	−12
Missouri	34	− 7
Range: (Alabama-Missouri)	31	16
Group II:		
Texas	24	−33
Louisiana	57	− 6
Arizona	63	−10
New Mexico	81	−10
Range: (Texas-New Mexico)	57	23
Group III:		
Oregon	24	− 5
Washington	32	+ 3
Nevada	40	+ 1
California	47	+ 8
Range: (Oregon-California)	23	13
Group IV:		
Idaho	14	0
Iowa	26	+ 5
Wyoming	30	+ 5
South Dakota	33	+ 6
Range: (Idaho-South Dakota)	19	6

[1] *Normal* is the Democratic percentage for each state based on the 1924–32 election results and corresponding to a national Democratic vote of 41 per cent.

nation is 55 per cent Democratic, for example, the injection of the religious issue, with a candidate as popular and able as Alfred Smith, would not necessarily cause the country to go Republican.

Religion as an issue in a political campaign did not appear for the first, or last, time in 1928. Another of many examples occurred in the Cleveland-Blaine campaign of 1884. Blaine expected Catholic support because his mother was a Catholic (and particularly Catholic Irish support because of his anti-British stand). It is said that Blaine failed to rebuke a Protestant minister who in an interview with Blaine referred to the Democratic Party "whose antecedents have been Rum, Romanism, and Rebellion," and that this failure cost him New York State, and so the election. (John D. Hicks: *The American Nation*, p. 204.)

The Democrats spread this story, adding that Blaine himself had made the distasteful remark. The election results bear out the historian's version of the effect of this use of prejudice in the campaign. On the basis of an analysis similar to that I made of the 1928 election, it is evident that the effect of "Rum, Romanism, and Rebellion" was not limited to New York alone. In a generally close election Cleveland benefited also by a few points in strongly Catholic New York, Connecticut, Massachusetts, and Illinois, but lost a few points in border and Southern states, such as Virginia and West Virginia.

The issue was not of great importance. Its influence can be measured in slight shifts of not more than 1 to 4 percentage points in either direction compared with 15 to 20 points in 1928. It does serve to corroborate our analysis of 1928, and further illustrates the consequences of religious feeling if injected in a close campaign. (Cleveland's victory over Blaine was a matter of only 23,000 votes, out of a total of nearly 10,000,000.)

That religious feeling and prejudice other than the anti-Catholic sentiment cited in these two studies have often appeared is illustrated in an example from Edward J. Flynn's *You're the Boss*. In describing the defeat of Joseph V. McKee by LaGuardia in a New York City mayoralty contest, he says (pp. 136–8):

> About ten days before the election a bombshell fell in the midst of our dwindling hopes. Samuel Untermeyer added the weight of his name and influence to the attack by LaGuardia on McKee, charging that McKee had libeled the Jewish people in an article he had published. . . . Anyone, either Jew or Gentile, who had

read the article as a whole would have recognized that it was fair
to the Jewish people. . . . LaGuardia, in making his attack, lifted
only the part that would seem to make McKee anti-Semitic and
Untermeyer, emotionally excited and abandoning his accustomed
logical reasoning, issued a statement attacking McKee on the
grounds of anti-Semitism. . . . It was evident that an immediate
reaction was setting in against McKee. . . . McKee's repeated
attempts to show that his entire life was a story of tolerance were
of no avail. Neither was a vigorous refutation of the attack by
Nathan Straus, Jr., himself a Jew. . . . The night the sad returns
came in our group was sitting around in a state of great dejection.
Herbert Bayard Swope pronounced the requiem: "We had the
best candidate, we had the best leaders, and we had the best
arguments. But the people would not believe us."

With these illustrations in mind, each drawn from dramatic
moments in our political history, we can appreciate more clearly
the comparisons between the political patterns of individual states
and that of the nation. My aim is to develop for every state a
normal relation to the national political cycle, and to do so we
must give special attention to abnormalities. For this reason the
particular regional abnormalities evident in the elections of 1896
and 1904, of 1916, 1940, and 1944, and of 1928 will appear again in
the following discussion of the records of fifteen electorally important states. Readers should check what they think they know
about the political behavior of their own states with the actual
history recorded in the next chapter. They will find many uses for
the record of the relation of each state to the national political
pattern. If they will be constantly on the alert for issues that may
distort local voting habits, they will see that as the nation goes, so
go their favorite states.

Chapter 10:

As Your State Goes, So Goes the Nation

Every presidential election brings Maine a certain kind of publicity to which other states are much more entitled. The old slogan: "As Maine goes, so goes the nation," is a hang-over from the days of Republican political tides. Politically, Maine is unique only because its election of state officials occurs in September, nearly two months before the presidential elections, and because it is predominantly Republican. Of course it goes as the nation whenever the nation is Republican, but not as a rule when the nation goes Democratic.

Actually, in the sense in which the relation between national and state political patterns is developed in these chapters, it is still correct to say: "As Maine goes, so goes the nation," or "As the nation goes, so goes Maine," but believe-it-or-not it is even more correct to say that:

As the nation goes,

So goes Massachusetts,
So goes New York,

So goes Pennsylvania,
So goes Illinois,
So goes Ohio,
So goes Michigan,
So goes Wisconsin,
So goes Minnesota,
So goes California,

and so goes almost any state outside the South. They are all at least as barometric as Maine—most of them more so. Anyone who wishes to gauge the national political temper by the temper of any state or section will do well to start, not with Maine, but with a more typical state like Pennsylvania, Ohio, Illinois, or Iowa.

This sweeping generalization will probably surprise anyone who has not read Chapter 7. It may even surprise many who have studied the state patterns and been impressed with the differences among them. But my generalization stands. It does not mean that they show identical Democratic or Republican percentages in all or most elections. Ohio is probably the one state in which more than any other the Democratic vote has approximated the actual national percentages, and even in this case identical percentages are few and far between.

For analytical as well as forecasting purposes, relationships between the national and state patterns fall into three types. In the first the two patterns tend to rise and fall together, but with fairly constant margins of differences between them. The state averages for either major party may remain uniformly above or below the national. Given the national average, it is necessary only to add or subtract the relatively stable differences in order to obtain an estimate of the state percentages. Given a state percentage, an estimate for the nation may be obtained by reversing the process.

In another type of relationship the state averages may fluctuate with the national, but more or less violently. In the third type the margin of difference between state and national averages may be gradually widening or diminishing over a period of years. These three types need to be recognized in making state forecasts from national indications, or national forecasts from state indications.

Massachusetts, New York, New Jersey, Pennsylvania, Illinois, Iowa, are examples of states that usually vote as the nation does

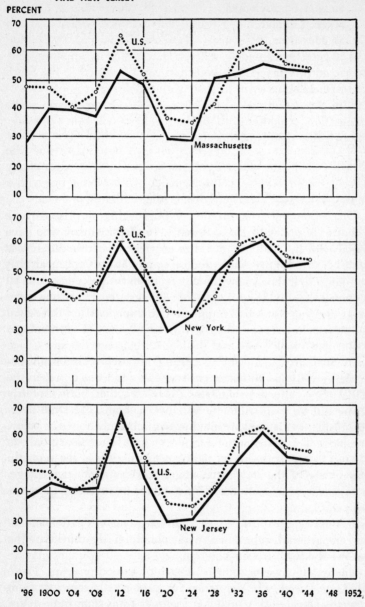

AS THE NATION GOES, SO GO MASSACHUSETTS, NEW YORK, AND NEW JERSEY

PERCENT

U.S.

Massachusetts

U.S.

New York

U.S.

New Jersey

'96 1900 '04 '08 '12 '16 '20 '24 '28 '32 '36 '40 '44 '48 1952

DEMOCRATIC PERCENTAGES OF TWO-PARTY VOTE FOR PRESIDENT

CHART 19

but on a lower Democratic level, with fairly stable margins of difference. Indiana and Missouri fluctuate less widely than the nation; Michigan, Wisconsin, Minnesota, California, Washington, and Oregon, more widely. Fifteen states, each an important battleground in every political election, are illustrated in the charts 19 to 23. Familiarity with their voting behavior compared with that of the nation should prove of value to students and politicians. Close attention to these simple charts will help the reader through the details of this chapter.

Massachusetts

Let us begin with Massachusetts. Its political record is compared with the national record in chart 19. We introduce it first both because it gives least promise as an illustration of similarity and because it shows how the discussion in the preceding chapter on issues that divide applies to individual states. Every one of the great dividing issues had pronounced and unmistakable effects on the Massachusetts presidential vote.

But if we look again and distinguish between the seven elections where national problems affected Massachusetts and the rest of the country in much the same manner, and the six where national issues affected the states differently, a pattern may take shape and we shall see method in this "madness." The validity of this distinction is demonstrated in two tables given below, one a comparison of Democratic percentages for Massachusetts and the United States in the seven more normal elections, the second a comparison of the six elections influenced by regional problems.

Normally Massachusetts is 7 percentage points less Democratic than the United States. In all but one of the seven normal elections the Democratic vote was 6.3 to 8.6 points below the national percentage. In the abnormal years (abnormal because of regional issues) the story is very different.

There was no consistent relationship between election results in Massachusetts and the nation for these six abnormal years. In 1896 the Democratic vote in Massachusetts was 19.8 points below, and in 1928, 9.3 points above the national percentage. If we allow for the normal difference, minus 7 points, we find (with apologies for oversimplification) that Bryan's silver program cut the Democratic vote by 12.8 points; Parker's opposition to Bryan's program added 6.1 points; the threat of a European war in 1916 added 3.7 points; the Catholic candidate in 1928 added 16.3 points; and the war in Europe in 1940 followed by our formal entry into the war in 1944 added 5.4 and 6.1 points.

Presidential Elections, Massachusetts and the U.S.
Group 1 (per cent Democratic)

	MASSACHUSETTS	UNITED STATES	DIFFERENCE
1900	39.7	46.8	− 7.1
1908	36.9	45.5	− 8.6
1912	52.8	64.4	−11.6
1920	28.9	36.1	− 7.2
1924	28.5	34.8	− 6.3
1932	52.1	59.1	− 7.0
1936	55.1	62.2	− 7.1

Average (excludes 1912) − 7.2

Presidential Elections, Massachusetts and the U.S.
Group 2 (per cent Democratic)

	MASSACHUSETTS	UNITED STATES	DIFFERENCE	ADJUSTED FOR NORMAL DIFF. OF− 7.0
1896	27.5	47.3	−19.8	−12.8
1904	39.1	40.0	− .9	+ 6.1
1916	48.0	51.7	− 3.7	+ 3.3
1928	50.5	41.2	+ 9.3	+16.3
1940	53.4	55.0	− 1.6	+ 5.4
1944	52.9	53.8	− .9	+ 6.1

Massachusetts is not permanently in the Democratic column merely because it has gone Democratic in all five elections since 1928. As a matter of fact, none of the conditions that raised the Democratic vote in the Bay State above 50 per cent existed in the early part of 1948. With the New Deal tide at a much lower level in 1948 than in 1932 and 1936, and without the supporting war factor of 1940 and 1944, Democrats can normally expect about 46 per cent of the two-party total or 7 points less than in 1944, assuming the two parties divide about as they did in 1944.

In no other state can we see so clearly how a normal difference between nation and state is enlarged or reduced by issues that have regional significance. The generalization: "As the nation goes, so goes Massachusetts," has to be qualified as often as not by the great sensitivity of this state to economic, religious, and other regional issues.

New York

"As the nation goes, so goes New York," from the appearance of the record in chart 19, is more plausible than the Massachusetts formula. Usually New York reflects the national mood at a Democratic level 2 to 3 points below the national. With an accurate appraisal of the political situation in New York, the mere addition of 2 to 3 points to the New York Democratic percentage automatically gives an estimate of the national strength of either major party.

In New York, as in Massachusetts, we should note the presidential elections in 1900, 1908, 1924, and the four elections from 1932 to 1944. Here, too, it is easy to see that opposition to Bryan's program cut the Democratic vote substantially in 1896, while in 1904 New York was even more Democratic than the nation, thanks to Parker.

In 1928 it is clear that a large bloc of Catholic votes for Alfred Smith, again as in Massachusetts, gave the Democrats an unusually large portion of the total vote. If the nation had gone 43 instead of 41 per cent Democratic in 1928, it is evident from chart 19 that Smith would have carried New York.

"As the nation goes, so goes New York," has been a good formula since 1932, but it should be noted that in the last two presidential elections the Democrats were supported by the Liberal and American Labor parties, which meant 7 additional percentage points in 1940, 13 in 1944. Without this support New York would have gone Republican in both elections.

Pennsylvania

As we go from New York through New Jersey to Pennsylvania, the relation between the national and state political patterns be-

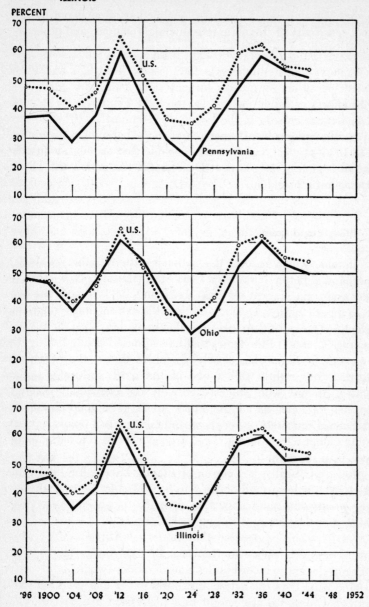

PERCENT

U.S.

Pennsylvania

U.S.

Ohio

U.S.

Illinois

'96 1900 '04 '08 '12 '16 '20 '24 '28 '32 '36 '40 '44 '48 1952

DEMOCRATIC PERCENTAGES OF TWO-PARTY VOTE FOR PRESIDENT

CHART 20

comes much more regular (chart 20). Pennsylvania has given the Democrats a smaller percentage of its votes than the United States in the last thirteen presidential elections, the margins varying between 5 and 12 points through 1932, 2 and 4 points since then. The state went Republican in 1932 (as in 1916, 1920, and 1924), but a considerably greater turnout since 1932, due partially to the efforts of labor unions, has brought Pennsylvania into the Democratic column in the last three elections. In 1944 the state was only 3 points less Democratic than the nation. On the basis of the 1936–44 elections, we may conclude that as long as Pennsylvania is at least 50 per cent Democratic, the nation will elect a Democratic president.

Illinois and Iowa

Illinois, which reflects the national pattern rather closely, is perhaps a better barometer than Massachusetts, New York, or Pennsylvania. Except for 1920, 1924, and 1928, Illinois has been 2 to 6 per cent less Democratic than the nation, and for the four elections from 1932 to 1944 the difference has been only 3 to 4 points. To most of the issues that have aroused strong feeling, the response of Illinois has closely resembled that of the nation and is therefore rightly called one of the most politically typical states. Anyone who gauges accurately the Democratic strength in that state can, by adding 3 to 4 points, get a good clue to the national Democratic percentage, and taking 3 to 4 points from the state's Republican strength get a good clue to the national Republican strength.

Iowa, politically, is a cousin of Illinois. Except for 1920, 1924, and 1932, it has usually been 7 to 8 points less Democratic than the country. Its political pattern since 1896 has been fairly typical of that of the nation, with two exceptions. In 1928 many old-time Iowa Republicans decided they preferred Alfred Smith's views on agricultural policy to Hoover's. In 1932 Iowa—for the only time in the entire record under consideration—went slightly more Democratic than the nation, obviously under duress of low farm prices. Unless we are caught in a depression like that of 1932, Iowa may be expected to go as the nation goes and remain about 7 points below the national Democratic level.

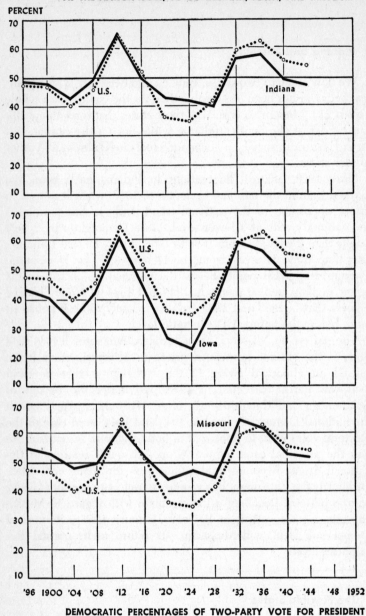

AS THE NATION GOES, SO GO INDIANA, IOWA, AND MISSOURI

PERCENT

U.S.

Indiana

U.S.

Iowa

Missouri

U.S.

'96 1900 '04 '08 '12 '16 '20 '24 '28 '32 '36 '40 '44 '48 1952

DEMOCRATIC PERCENTAGES OF TWO-PARTY VOTE FOR PRESIDENT

CHART 21

Indiana and Missouri

We now come to two states, Indiana and Missouri, where political behavior has been less flexible than for the country as a whole (chart 21). Missouri is typical of those states that form the northern border of the South. Indiana, while not on the border, has strong historical, social, and economic roots in Kentucky and other border states.

Since 1920, political fluctuations in Indiana have been less marked than in the national cycle. Since 1928, when it moved in direct opposition to the national trend, Indiana has paralleled the national cycle, at a lower level. More Democratic by 2 to 4 points than the nation from 1896 to 1908, it may be that Indiana's long-time trend is away from the Democrats. The Democratic average dropped 3 points below the national in 1932, 5 points below in 1936, and 6 points in 1940 and 1944. One may hazard a guess that in 1948 and 1952 Indiana is likely to be 6 points or more below the national Democratic level.

The pattern in Missouri, as in Indiana, fluctuates less widely than in the nation. Low farm prices in Missouri, as in Iowa, caused an abnormal swing to the Democratic side in 1932. This was partly corrected in 1936, and under the impact of isolationism and the third-term issue Missouri dropped below the national Democratic level in 1940 and 1944, even though the electoral votes went to Roosevelt in both elections. If isolationism was the principal cause of that drop, Missouri's relation to the national trend becomes quite uncertain for 1948 and 1952. Ordinarily the state might be expected to reflect the national Democratic pattern. Recalling a like problem with regard to Massachusetts, we may ask if in 1948–52 Missouri rises to its normal Democratic level, will Massachusetts return to its normal Republican level?

The Flexible States

The next four states belong to that group of Northern and Western states which are more flexible politically than the rest of

AS THE NATION GOES, SO GO MICHIGAN, WISCONSIN, AND MINNESOTA

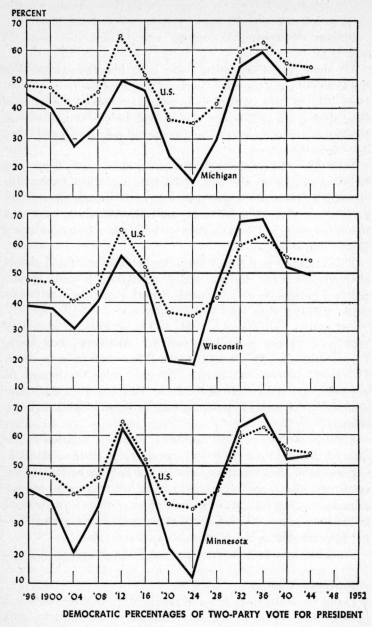

PERCENT

U.S.

Michigan

U.S.

Wisconsin

U.S.

Minnesota

'96 1900 '04 '08 '12 '16 '20 '24 '28 '32 '36 '40 '44 '48 1952

DEMOCRATIC PERCENTAGES OF TWO-PARTY VOTE FOR PRESIDENT

CHART 22

the nation. From this group, which extends from Michigan northwest and to the Pacific coast, I have selected for illustration Michigan, Wisconsin, Minnesota, and California (charts 22 and 23).

Michigan, like Pennsylvania, has been less Democratic than the nation through the whole period, but during the four elections from 1932 to 1944 its vote more nearly resembled the national than during the 1920's and the period before World War I. Michigan in recent elections has fluctuated only 3 to 5 points below the national level.

Politically, Wisconsin and Minnesota, since 1928, have been twice as flexible as the nation. In 1932 and 1936 Democratic strength in both states was proportionately greater than in the nation, but after 1936 fell more abruptly. Wisconsin and Minnesota, in short, follow the nation—whether in a Democratic or a Republican direction.

This disparity in political flexibility between state and nation, characteristic of the Northern and Western states, signifies greater political independence and freedom from Republican or Democratic tradition than exist in the older sections of the country. Third parties have found a ready following here. Wisconsin in 1924 gave 54 per cent of its vote to LaFollette's Progressive Party; Minnesota, 41 per cent; North Dakota, 45 per cent; South Dakota, 37 per cent; Washington, 36 per cent; and California, 33 per cent. The Roosevelt Bull Moose Party of 1912 took over practically the entire Republican vote in South Dakota and California.

Because of their political flexibility, election-campaign strategists and political commentators usually consider these states as unpredictable. But this designation is not justified by the statistical record. They vote as does the nation, but political issues that cause, say, a 5-point shift in Democratic-Republican percentages in the Eastern and North Central states will cause a corresponding 10-point shift in the Northwest and Pacific states.

We have seen that as New York or Pennsylvania goes, so go New Jersey, Illinois, and Iowa. We can now add: as Minnesota goes, so goes California.

Let us recall the three types of relationships between state and nation. Maine is an outstanding example of the third type, in which the relationship between state and national behavior

AS THE NATION GOES, SO GO WASHINGTON, OREGON, AND CALIFORNIA

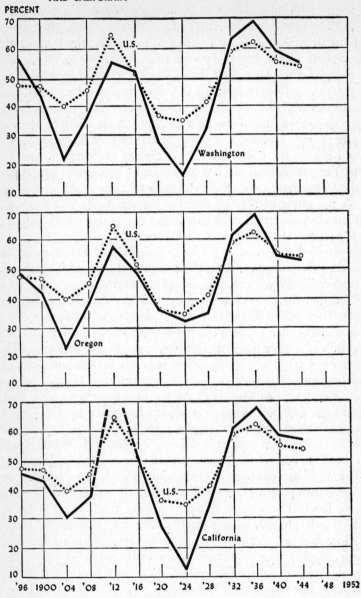

DEMOCRATIC PERCENTAGES OF TWO-PARTY VOTE FOR PRESIDENT

CHART 23

changes with time. Before 1912, Maine's Democratic percentage was 10 to 18 points below that of the nation. In 1912, when many Maine Republicans joined the Bull Moose Party, the Democratic proportion of the two-party vote rose so sharply as to top the national figure. After 1912, the Democratic trend in Maine reflected the national trend, but at a steadily decreasing level, and in 1936 had fallen nearly 20 points below the national level. Recognition of this downward trend made it possible, on the basis of the September 1936 gubernatorial election in Maine (which gave the Democrats 40 per cent of the vote), to predict that the presidential election two months later could go 60 per cent Democratic (the actual vote was 62.2 per cent).

In the spring of 1940 I pointed to the possibility that this drift might alter abruptly; until that happened Maine could serve as a barometric state. In May 1940, before the impending war issues had divided the country, a Gallup poll showed Maine to be 36 per cent Democratic. Taking the accuracy of the poll for granted, I added the 20-point margin according to my formula and predicted that the Democrats would poll 56 per cent of the nation's vote. They polled 55 per cent in the election in November.

An elaboration of Maine's barometric qualifications may be worth while, since this state illustrates remarkably well the problems involved in predicting future behavior on the basis of past relationships. The 1936 correspondence between Maine and the nation still held in May 1940. As the campaign got under way, the war in Europe and growing concern over the role to be played by the United States altered the picture. The margin between Maine and the nation narrowed from 19 points in 1936 to 6 points in 1944, a shift of 10 points toward the national Democratic level. Will the elections of 1948 and 1952 disclose whether in postwar campaigns Maine will return to the usual lower Democratic level? The same problem, of course, exists in all states in which a shift to either party resulted from the international crisis.

How shall we summarize these nation-state relationships? For those readers who remember more easily what they see, the graphic record for the forty-eight states in Chapter 8 and the charts in this chapter will be helpful.

It may be useful to summarize by answering the question: if the national vote is evenly divided between Democrats and Republicans, how many and which states would go Democratic and which Republican? How would this list be altered if the national vote is 54 or 58 per cent Democratic?

On the basis of the shift from the depths of the Republican tide 1920–4 to the crest of the Democratic tide in 1936 I have computed the expected Democratic percentages for each state if the nation goes 50, 54, and 58 per cent Democratic. I have divided the states into two groups. The first includes the twenty-two states which are more than 50 per cent Democratic when the nation is evenly divided, and so may be regarded as typically Democratic. The other twenty-six may be looked upon as typically Republican.

In addition to the Solid South the typically Democratic group includes five border states, Maryland, Virginia, West Virginia, Kentucky, and Missouri, two Southwestern states, New Mexico and Arizona, and three additional Western states, Nevada, Oregon, and Montana. Idaho misses falling into this group by half a point.

When the nation goes 50 to 58 per cent Democratic, these states will ordinarily be found in the Democratic column, but at different levels. In the Southeastern states the Democratic vote is usually 20 to 49 per cent higher than in the nation. (Republican votes in South Carolina and Mississippi are "scarcer than hen's teeth," according to the record.) Three border states, Virginia, North Carolina, and Tennessee, and also Arizona, are 10 to 20 points above the national Democratic percentage. All the rest, chiefly border and Western states, are 1 to 10 points above.

Political analysis and prediction would be simple if states that normally go Republican when the popular vote is evenly divided stayed Republican, as the Southern states stay Democratic. But of the twenty-six states listed as Republican when the nation is 50 per cent Democratic, only ten are reasonably certain to remain Republican when the nation is 54 per cent Democratic. Only Maine, New Hampshire, and Vermont are likely to stay in the Republican fold when the nation is 59 per cent Democratic, as in 1932.

Only two states, Maine and Vermont, normally drop below the national Democratic percentage by more than 10 points, and about seven by 5 to 10 points. The rest tend normally to fall below the national figure by less than 5 points. When the country is 58 per cent Democratic, the more flexible states, Idaho, Washington,

California, Wisconsin, North Dakota, and Minnesota, exceed the national percentage by 1 to 3 points.

Democratic Percentages of Two-Party Votes
For (26) States Predominantly Republican
(when the nation goes 50, 54, and 58 per cent Democratic)

	DEMOCRATIC PER CENT			DIFFERENCE		
U.S.	50	54	58	50	54	58
Ind.	50	53	55	0	− 1	− 3
Idaho	49	55	60	− 1	+ 1	+ 2
Colo.	49	53	57	− 1	− 1	− 1
Ohio	49	53	57	− 1	− 1	− 1
Del.	49	52	54	− 1	− 2	− 4
Nebr.	48	51	55	− 2	− 3	− 3
Wash.	47	54	61	− 3	0	+ 3
Wyo.	47	52	57	− 3	− 2	− 1
R.I.	47	50	53	− 3	− 4	− 5
Calif.	46	53	60	− 4	− 1	+ 2
N.J.	46	51	55	− 4	− 3	− 3
N.Y.	46	50	54	− 4	− 4	− 4
Conn.	46	50	54	− 4	− 4	− 4
Wis.	45	53	60	− 5	− 1	+ 2
N.Dak.	45	53	61	− 5	− 1	+ 3
Ill.	45	49	54	− 5	− 5	− 4
N.H.	45	47	49	− 5	− 7	− 9
Minn.	44	51	59	− 6	− 3	+ 1
Pa.	43	48	53	− 7	− 6	− 5
Kans.	43	47	50	− 7	− 7	− 8
Mass.	43	47	51	− 7	− 7	− 7
Iowa	42	46	51	− 8	− 8	− 7
S.Dak.	41	46	51	− 9	− 8	− 7
Mich.	41	47	53	− 9	− 7	− 5
Maine	36	38	40	−14	−16	−18
Vt.	33	36	39	−17	−18	−19

The systematic normal relationships between individual states, and between state and nation, can be put to many practical uses. We have already seen how easily the effect of a major political issue in the election of an individual state can be measured on the basis of departures from normal voting behavior. I have also indicated that on the basis of normal relations we can translate the political behavior of any state into an appraisal of the national political balance. Determining which way the nation goes on this or any other basis does not necessarily tell us which party will win a given presidential election, for the division of the electoral votes may not correspond with the division of the popular vote.

Democratic Percentages of Two-Party Votes
For (22) States Predominantly Democratic
(when the nation goes 50, 54, and 58 per cent Democratic)

	DEMOCRATIC PER CENT			DIFFERENCES		
U.S.	50	54	58	50	54	58
S.C.	98	98	99	+48	+44	+41
Miss.	93	94	95	+43	+40	+37
Ga.	82	84	86	+32	+30	+28
La.	82	84	86	+32	+30	+28
Tex.	82	84	86	+32	+30	+28
Ala.	79	82	82	+29	+28	+27
Ark.	74	77	79	+24	+23	+21
Fla.	72	73	75	+22	+19	+17
N.C.	67	69	71	+17	+15	+13
Va.	67	68	69	+17	+14	+11
Tenn.	61	64	66	+11	+10	+ 8
Ariz.	60	64	68	+10	+10	+10
Okla.	59	62	65	+ 9	+ 8	+ 7
Utah	56	60	65	+ 6	+ 6	+ 7
Nev.	56	62	67	+ 6	+ 8	+ 9
N. Mex.	55	58	60	+ 5	+ 4	+ 2
Ky.	55	56	58	+ 5	+ 2	0
Ind.	55	57	60	+ 5	+ 3	+ 2
Mo.	54	56	59	+ 4	+ 2	+ 1
Mont.	54	60	66	+ 4	+ 6	+ 8
W. Va.	54	56	58	+ 4	+ 2	0
Oreg.	53	58	63	+ 3	+ 4	+ 5

Because a Democratic candidate receives such a large proportion of his electoral votes from the South, he must poll more than 50 per cent of the national vote to gain a majority of electoral votes.

The purpose of this chapter has been to familiarize the reader with the fact that for a series of national voting percentages there is a comparable series for his favorite state. The first corollary is that for any particular national percentage there is a comparable percentage for each of the forty-eight states. The second corollary is that the column of forty-eight state percentages automatically divides the corresponding electoral vote between the two major parties, those with percentages exceeding 50 going to the Democratic side, and those with less than 50 to the Republican. Upon these facts the reader can build an estimate of state popular and electoral votes from the nation's vote, and, with proper caution, he can estimate the national vote from the voting behavior of his favorite state. Out of these facts is built in the next chapter the schedule of popular and electoral votes required for estimating the outcome of presidential elections.

Chapter 11:

Who Gets the Electoral Votes?

If the reader likes statistics and at the same time earns his living as a national or local statesman, or heads an organization that rings doorbells and influences votes, or is just an average voter interested in the outcome of an election, he has doubtless already tried his hand at what this chapter undertakes to do. He has lined up the forty-eight states, checking off those certain to go Democratic no matter what the Republicans do and those likely to vote Republican no matter what the Democrats do, and finally those uncertain states where the outcome of the election will really be determined—where political strategy and effort are called for.

This state-by-state appraisal would not be vital if our founding fathers had provided for the election of presidents by a majority of the popular vote. In that event political strategy aimed at capturing key states would be considerably altered and the art of predicting elections greatly simplified. Under the present system, however, we cast our votes not for a candidate of a party but for electors to the electoral college. (The total number of electors according to the formula provided in the Constitution is 531, the sum of the seats in the House, 435, and in the Senate, 96.)

The votes of all electors from a state go to the party receiving the popular majority in that state, whether it is one vote (in which case the opposition would undoubtedly contest the election) or hundreds of thousands. The electoral system often results in a lack of correspondence between the popular vote and the electoral vote for president.

Two Presidents, Hayes in 1876, and Harrison in 1888, came to office with less than a majority of the two-party vote. Sometimes candidates received practically the entire electoral vote of the nation, quite out of relation to their popular vote. The Republicans in 1928, for example, cast 21 million votes, the Democrats 15 millions; but Hoover received 444 electoral votes, and Alfred E. Smith 87. Hoover, supported by 59 per cent of the popular vote, had 84 per cent of the electoral vote. Twelve years later, in 1940, the Democrats cast 27 million votes and the Republicans 22 million, but Roosevelt won 449 electoral votes and Willkie only 82. Supported by 60 per cent of the popular vote, Roosevelt won 85 per cent of the electoral vote.

✓ The lack of correspondence between the popular and the electoral vote given to presidential candidates, however, does not mean that there is no systematic relationship between them. As a matter of fact, since there is a normal relationship between a party's popular vote in the nation and in each state, there must of necessity be a similar relationship between its popular vote and the national electoral vote. We should be able to improve on the usual rough-and-ready method of estimating electoral votes a candidate may be expected to receive for a given popular vote in the nation.

No longer content with grouping the states as definitely Democratic, definitely Republican, and uncertain, we can, on the basis of our systematic analysis of the 1916–44 experience, proceed to a more exact method of appraising the uncertain states. The first step is to draw up a more complete table than that on page 120, with the national Democratic percentages entered across the top, ranging from 48 to 60, and the left column listing the forty-eight states. We then enter opposite each state under each national Democratic percentage the corresponding state percentage. We

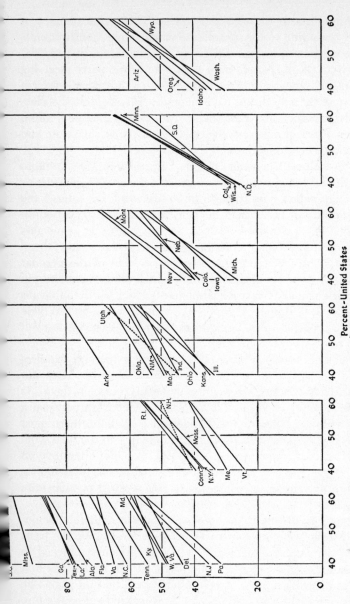

Percent—United States

RELATION OF THE NATIONAL DEMOCRATIC PERCENTAGE OF THE TWO-PARTY VOTE TO THE DEMOCRATIC PERCENTAGE FOR EACH STATE (based on experience of 1916–44)

When the nation votes 40 per cent Democratic, only Southern states vote more than 50 per cent Democratic. When the nation is 60 per cent Democratic, all states except Maine and Vermont tend to go Democratic. For a 10-point increase or decrease in the national Democratic percentage, the Southern states shift less than 10 points and the Northwestern and Far Western shift about twice as much.

will identify those columns by "U.S. 48," "U.S. 50," etc. (The reader will do well at this point to turn to the appendix, pp. 186–7, for this complete table, as well as to Chart 24, which is based on that table.)

In "U.S. 48" we find old friends, the twenty-two Southern states —still more than 50 per cent Democratic. The electoral votes of these states would go, of course, to the Democratic candidate. In "U.S. 50," Indiana appears; in "U.S. 52," five more states, Idaho, Washington, Ohio, Delaware, and Colorado, join the ranks. By the time we reach "U.S. 60," all states but two—Maine and Vermont—have voted more than 50 per cent Democratic. In short as the nation goes from 48 to 60 per cent Democratic, the number of states more than 50 per cent Democratic increases from 22 to 46.

The next step is to prepare a simple table in which the number of electoral votes is substituted wherever a state percentage exceeds 50 per cent. The final step is to find the total electoral votes in each column, and this is what we get:

Normal Number of Electoral Votes Corresponding to National Popular Vote

(Based on elections of 1916–44)

U.S. PER CENT DEMOCRATIC	ELECTORAL VOTES DEMOCRATIC	REPUBLICAN
35	127	404
40	148	383
45	191	340
48	204	327
49	204	327
50	217	314
51	221	310
52	263	268
53	313	218
54	399	132
55	427	104
56	462	69
57	481	50
58	519	12
59	519	12
60	523	8

This schedule of popular and electoral votes furnishes several surprises. When the popular vote is evenly divided, as in "U.S. 50," the Democrats can expect only the 217 electoral votes from the twenty-two Democratic states, 49 short of the minimum of 266, and the Republicans would win handsomely. Even with 52 per cent of the popular vote the Democrats can lose, since their share of the electoral votes is only 263, or 3 short. Only when the Democrats have at least 53 per cent of the popular vote is victory certain.

Another surprising fact revealed by the table is that for every point in the popular vote above 52 per cent, the Democratic electoral votes increase sharply, reaching a total of 519 when the popular vote is divided 58 per cent Democratic and 42 per cent Republican. In a Republican landslide, when the Democrats receive only 35 per cent of the popular vote, 10 of the 22 states normally Democratic would shift to the Republican side, leaving 12 Southern states—127 electoral votes—in the Democratic column. In other words, because of the relatively inflexible political allegiance in the South, the Democratic Party can practically bank on a minimum of 127 electoral votes under almost any circumstances (except when a deep-cutting issue like the religious issue of 1928 appears in the campaign). At the other extreme we find that only three states, Maine, New Hampshire, and Vermont, are inflexibly Republican.

When the nation is apparently evenly divided, shrewd political maneuvering for electoral votes is required; a real battle for the presidency is on. Let us assume that the Democratic proportion of the two-party vote rises, point by point, from 50 to 60 per cent. Which blocks of states will then appear, one after another, in the Democratic column? At the 50 per cent level, Indiana may barely edge in to increase the Democratic total to 217, 49 short of a majority. It does this in column "50" in the next table.

At this stage the Democrats could aim at one of several combinations to secure the additional votes. They could endeavor to secure the contiguous states, New York (47 votes) and New Jersey (16 votes). Winning these, their candidate would be elected with a narrow margin of 14 votes. Or they could woo Pennsylvania (36) and Ohio (26) and, if successful, win with a surplus of 13 votes. If they could carry Ohio (26) and Illinois

The Popular and Electoral Vote (Based on Experience of 8 Presidential Elections, 1916–44)

STATE	ELEC-TORAL VOTES	DEMOCRATIC ELECTORAL VOTES, WHEN THE DEMOCRATIC PERCENTAGE OF THE U.S. TWO-PARTY VOTE IS:												
		48	49	50	51	52	53	54	55	56	57	58	59	60
UNITED STATES	531													
Maine	5													
Vermont	3													
New Hampshire	4													4
Iowa	10											10	.	.
Kansas	8											8	.	.
Massachusetts	16											16	.	.
South Dakota	4											4	.	.
Michigan	19										19	.	.	.
Pennsylvania	35									35	.	.	.	.
Illinois	28								28	.	.	.	.	.
New York	47							47	.	.	.	.	.	.
Connecticut	8							8	.	.	.	.	.	.
Minnesota	11							11	.	.	.	.	.	.
New Jersey	16							16	.	.	.	.	.	.
Rhode Island	4							4	.	.	.	.	.	.
California	25						25	.	.	.	.	.	.	.
Nebraska	6						6	.	.	.	.	.	.	.
North Dakota	4						4	.	.	.	.	.	.	.
Wisconsin	12						12	.	.	.	.	.	.	.
Wyoming	3						3	.	.	.	.	.	.	.
Colorado	6					6	.	.	.	.	.	.	.	.
Delaware	3					3	.	.	.	.	.	.	.	.
Ohio	25					25	.	.	.	.	.	.	.	.
Washington	8					8	.	.	.	.	.	.	.	.
Idaho	4				4	.	.	.	.	.	.	.	.	.
Indiana	13			13	.	.	.	.	.	.	.	.	.	.
Alabama	11	11	.	.	.	.	.	.	.	.	.	.	.	.
Arizona	4	4	.	.	.	.	.	.	.	.	.	.	.	.
Arkansas	9	9	.	.	.	.	.	.	.	.	.	.	.	.
Florida	8	8	.	.	.	.	.	.	.	.	.	.	.	.
Georgia	12	12	.	.	.	.	.	.	.	.	.	.	.	.
Kentucky	11	11	.	.	.	.	.	.	.	.	.	.	.	.
Louisiana	10	10	.	.	.	.	.	.	.	.	.	.	.	.
Maryland	8	8	.	.	.	.	.	.	.	.	.	.	.	.
Mississippi	9	9	.	.	.	.	.	.	.	.	.	.	.	.
Missouri	15	15	.	.	.	.	.	.	.	.	.	.	.	.
Montana	4	4	.	.	.	.	.	.	.	.	.	.	.	.
Nevada	3	3	.	.	.	.	.	.	.	.	.	.	.	.
New Mexico	4	4	.	.	.	.	.	.	.	.	.	.	.	.
North Carolina	14	14	.	.	.	.	.	.	.	.	.	.	.	.
Oklahoma	10	10	.	.	.	.	.	.	.	.	.	.	.	.
Oregon	6	6	.	.	.	.	.	.	.	.	.	.	.	.
South Carolina	8	8	.	.	.	.	.	.	.	.	.	.	.	.
Tennessee	12	12	.	.	.	.	.	.	.	.	.	.	.	.
Texas	23	23	.	.	.	.	.	.	.	.	.	.	.	.
Utah	4	4	.	.	.	.	.	.	.	.	.	.	.	.
Virginia	11	11	.	.	.	.	.	.	.	.	.	.	.	.
West Virginia	8	8	.	.	.	.	.	.	.	.	.	.	.	.
Total		204	204	217	221	263	313	399	427	462	481	519	519	523

(29), they would assure their candidate of a majority of 6 votes. Instead of these combinations, they could try for the politically flexible states of Wisconsin (12), Minnesota (11), Washington (8), and California (25), and win with a margin of 7 votes. These are some of the possible combinations.

In reality, only a few combinations are within the realm of practicability. The order in which states would be likely to join the Democratic ranks as the Democratic proportion of the national popular vote rises above 50 per cent is as follows:

"U.S. 51," only one additional state, Idaho (4).

"U.S. 52," four states, Washington (8), Ohio (25), Delaware (3), and Colorado (6)—raising the Democratic total to 263.

"U.S. 53," five states, Wyoming (31), Wisconsin (12), North Dakota (4), Nebraska (4), and California (25)—bringing victory to the Democrats with 313 electoral votes, or 47 to spare.

Thus the break-even point for the Democrats lies between 52 and 53 per cent of the popular vote (chart 25).

From this point on, the Democratic electoral gains for each point-rise in their share of the popular vote mount rapidly as they win states with large populations and correspondingly large electoral votes, such as New York, Pennsylvania, Ohio, California, and Illinois.

By the time the national Democratic level reaches 58 per cent, only three states hold out against a landslide like that of 1936—Maine, New Hampshire, and Vermont.

Even New Hampshire joins when the country goes 60 per cent Democratic, but Maine and Vermont are as steadfastly Republican in a Democratic victory as twelve Southern states are solidly Democratic in a Republican victory.

If the Democratic strategists can launch a campaign on a foundation of about 200 electoral votes, which ordinarily have been theirs in the elections of 1932 to 1944, then their main attack will be leveled at certain prize states with large electoral votes and flexible behavior. Some are easier to win than others. The most important will be found in these columns:

In "U.S. 52" is Ohio, with 25 votes.

In "U.S. 53," California with 25.

In "U.S. 54," New Jersey with 16, and New York (the greatest prize of all) with 47 votes.

In "U.S. 55," Illinois with 28.

In "U.S. 56," Pennsylvania with 35.
In "U.S. 57," Michigan with 19.

Except for Missouri and Texas, this list contains all the states with 15 or more electoral votes.

If the Democrats made sure of Ohio ("U.S. 52") and California ("U.S. 53"), they might barely win. But if they reach into the 54 per cent level and take New Jersey (16 votes) or New York (47), victory would be more certain. Perhaps the thing that strikes us most forcibly in studying this prize list is that the Democrats could lose New York, Illinois, Pennsylvania, Michigan, and Massachusetts and still win the election provided they secured New Jersey, California, and Ohio and made doubly sure of a few additional Northern states in the 52–53 per cent columns and of course provided the 22 normally Southern states all stay within the Democratic fold.

These speculations on the relationship between the electoral and the popular vote are based on the normal correspondence between the national and the state patterns for the 1916–44 period. There is naturally no guarantee that the patterns in the 1948 and subsequent elections will resemble the patterns we have traced in the 1920's and 1930's. It is necessary to allow for the development of abnormal events even if what they might be and what effect they might have on elections cannot be foreseen. It is possible and desirable, however, to compare the actual number of electoral votes obtained by the Republicans or Democrats in each of the eight elections from 1916 to 1944 with the number they should have obtained according to our schedule. A guide to future possible discrepancies may be found in the extent to which the peculiar issues and situations in 1940, 1944, and 1928 caused the electoral vote to depart from normal.

Chart 25 shows the normal schedule of popular and electoral votes compared with the actual votes of 1916–44, and therefore the discrepancies between them. The schedule of normal electoral expectations is indicated by the curve, the actual Democratic electoral votes by the crosses (x) labeled according to the election years they represent (1912, 1916, etc.), and the discrepancies may be seen at a glance. The Democratic electoral vote in 1928 was nearly 70 votes below normal, a discrepancy accounted for by the 67 electoral votes of Kentucky, Virginia, North

THE "BREAK-EVEN" POINT IN PRESIDENTIAL ELECTIONS

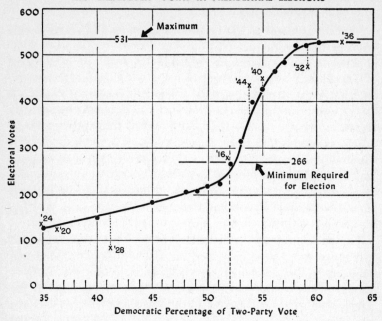

RELATION OF DEMOCRATIC PERCENTAGE OF TWO-PARTY VOTE FOR
PRESIDENT AND THE NUMBER OF DEMOCRATIC ELECTORAL VOTES

A Democratic candidate must have something more than
52 per cent of the two-party popular vote to receive the
required minimum of 266 electoral votes. The excess over
266 mounts rapidly as the popular vote rises from 52 to 58
per cent.

CHART 25.

Carolina, Florida, and Texas that went to Hoover as a result of
anti-Catholic feeling.

With the country at war in 1944, the Democratic electoral vote
exceeded normal by 33. Will the Republicans regain those votes
in 1948 or 1952? What states would be involved?

The Republicans would regain the ground lost in the Eastern
and Far Western states, and the Democrats recover strength lost
in the Central states as a result of war. The electoral votes of only
twelve states would be switched. Seven of the twelve, with 69
electoral votes—normally Democratic—went Republican in 1944:
Colorado, Indiana, Nebraska, North Dakota, Ohio, Wisconsin,
and Wyoming. The other five, with 102 electoral votes, Illinois,
Massachusetts, Michigan, New Hampshire, and Pennsylvania—
normally Republican—shifted to the Democrats in 1944. A return
to normal, with the country 54 per cent Democratic, would deprive the Democrats of 33 electoral votes. This alone would not
jeopardize the Democratic margin. If doubtful New York—normally only 50.3 per cent Democratic in "U.S. 54"—were also to
shift, and the Democratic electoral vote fell from 399 to 319, the
Democrats would still have a fairly safe margin.

*Effect of Abnormal Voting in 1944 on Democratic Electoral
Votes*

STATE	1944 DEMOCRATIC PERCENTAGE		1944 ELECTORAL VOTES	
	ACTUAL	NORMAL	ACTUAL	NORMAL
U.S.	54	54	432	399)
Colorado	47	53	—	6
Illinois	52	49	28	—
Indiana	47	53	—	13
Massachusetts	53	47	16	—
Michigan	51	47	19	—
Nebraska	41	51	—	6
New Hampshire	52	47	4	—
North Dakota	46	53	—	4
Ohio	50	53	—	25
Pennsylvania	51	48	35	—
Wisconsin	49	53	—	12
Wyoming	49	53	—	3
Total			102	69

Of the historical issues that could distort the normal line-up of electoral votes in 1948 and 1952, we can not yet rule out religion and war. Some serious economic split, like that caused by the silver issue, could arise, but we have no way of anticipating it. If such an economic problem were to develop and were recognized in time, our ample information on the economic groups that would be affected would enable us to determine the political reaction we could expect in the various states.

Another upsetting factor in the shape of a third party could appear in 1952, but unless it is an outgrowth of the 1948 third party there would be little information on which to base an estimate of the popular or electoral vote it would attract from Republicans or Democrats. Yet it is important to study the possible effect of a third party on the normal two-party schedule of popular and electoral votes.

Two or three illustrations will indicate some of the problems involved. Let us take the situation as it appeared at the beginning of 1948, when national sentiment seemed to run about 54 per cent Democratic and 46 per cent Republican, as in 1944. In judging how a third party might alter that balance, we must consider the popularity of the two major candidates, the possible strength of the third party, and what proportion of its votes would be drawn from each major party. In April 1948, forecasters of the impending election were faced with a choice of assumptions. Polls indicated that the third-party strength amounted to about 8 per cent, but sentiment for Truman ranged from 45 per cent of two-party sentiment if Dewey were his opponent to 54 per cent if Taft were his opponent.

If the two-party balance after the nominating convention records 54 per cent Democratic and 46 per cent Republican, what proportion of the total vote must a third party control in order to upset that balance?

Our schedule of popular and electoral votes indicates that a Republican candidate normally can win if the vote for the Democratic candidate does not exceed his by 8 per cent. (Note that the *break-even* point in the two-party balance, 52 per cent Democratic and 48 per cent Republican, means that the Democratic vote is 4 points or 8 per cent greater than the Republican vote.) Therefore, if the popularity of the Republican candidate is 46 per cent, he could expect to win if the Democratic candidate receives no more than 50 per cent (46 × 108). Consequently, if a third party draws 4 per cent of the total vote entirely from the Democratic candidate's 54 per cent, Republican victory would normally be assured.

Suppose the Democratic candidate's popularity is 60 per cent and the Republican's 40. In that case the Republican could win if the Democratic percentage were pulled down to 43 (40 × 108), and the third party's entire strength (17 per cent) came from the Democratic side.

Obviously, if the third party draws its support from both parties, its total strength would have to be greater to produce the above results. In our 54–46 illustration, for example, if the third party drew as much as 2 per cent from the Republican candidate, reducing his percentage to 44, the Republican could still win if the Democratic candidate received no more than 47.5 per cent (44 × 108). The third party in this case would have to draw 8 per cent of the total national vote—6 per cent from the Democrats and 2 from the Republicans.

These illustrations assume that the third party does not affect the usual balance among the states, but draws its support proportionately from all sections and groups. We have already observed, however, that third-party experience varies widely. Its strength may be twice as great in the East and Northwestern states as in the rest of the country. Furthermore, the effect of a third party with, say, 12 per cent of the total vote would have one effect in New York and Pennsylvania, where sentiment is 52 per cent Democratic, and quite another effect in a state like Montana—60 per cent Democratic. If a third party draws 12 per cent of the vote in Montana, one third from the Republicans and two thirds from the Democrats, the two-party balance would still be predominantly Democratic. (60 per cent Democratic and 40 per cent Republican becomes 51 Democratic, 37 Republican, and 12 third party.) But in New York a third-party vote of 12 per cent, with a third drawn from the Republicans and two thirds from the Democrats, would bring a Republican victory. (52 per cent Democratic and 48 Republican would become 43 Democratic, 45 Republican, and 12 third party.)

Obviously, the narrower the margin between the two major parties, the greater the power of a third party provided its strength is drawn more heavily from Republicans than Democrats.

The most probable balance between the two major parties in 1948–52, which is projected in the last chapter, is not nearly as one-sided as that which prevailed in 1924 (35 per cent Democratic), when LaFollette launched his campaign, or in 1912 (59 per cent Democratic), when Theodore Roosevelt launched his party. In many states the two major parties may be so nearly balanced that a third party, even with little support, could have decisive influence.

Even greater caution than usual is required in using our schedule of popular and electoral votes, particularly for those states in which the Democrats can expect only 51 to 54 per cent of the two-party vote. In 1944, when the nation voted 54 per cent Democratic, the following states went 51 to 54 per cent Democratic and provided 227 electoral votes for Roosevelt:

	1944 PER CENT DEMOCRATIC	ELECTORAL VOTES
Connecticut	53	8
Idaho	52	4
Illinois	52	28
Maryland	52	8
Massachusetts	53	16
Michigan	51	19
Minnesota	53	11
Missouri	52	15
New Hampshire	52	4
New Jersey	51	16
New Mexico	54	4
New York	52	47
Pennsylvania	51	35
Total		227

These close states would be potential political battlegrounds since they could all be shifted to the Republican column by a third-party vote of no more than 8 per cent of the total, provided the third party draws no more than a third of its strength from the Republicans.

The foregoing tabulation contains the reason why the Wallace third party appeared such a real threat to the Democrats in early

1948. In all these states except New Mexico the Democratic margin over the Republicans was only 6 points (53–47) in Connecticut, Massachusetts, and Minnesota; only 4 points in Idaho, Illinois, Maryland, Missouri, New Hampshire, and New York; and only 2 points in Michigan, New Jersey, and Pennsylvania. In 1944 the Democrats won with 432 electoral votes, giving a surplus of 166 that would disappear if these states were to swing to the Republican side as the result of a third-party vote of only 6 to 8 per cent.

Having gone this far with the political arithmetic involved in figuring who gets the majority of electoral votes in a given election, some readers may decide that perhaps, after all, the old rough-and-ready method of lining up the certain states and guessing the rest is good enough. I sympathize with that feeling. I recall several excellent predictions of electoral votes in 1944 made by the very simple method of reducing the 1940 Democratic percentages by 2 points. The central purpose of this book, however, is to demonstrate the rhyme and reason in the vast array of political facts—that measurable political patterns affected by domestic and international influences lie behind our final choice of presidents by the electoral rather than the popular vote.

Chapter 12:

Predict If You Must

Predicting elections, I feel reasonably sure, is going to be a favorite pastime during the next movement of the political tide. Those who wish to engage in that art or sport may find helpful a few of my experiences with both long-range and short-range predictions during the course of the New Deal tide. Among long-range predictions I include those made eighteen months in advance of the national election by means of an unpublicized formula: "As Kelly goes, so goes the nation"—amended in 1947 to "As Kennelly goes, so goes the nation"; among the medium-range forecasts I include predictions of congressional and presidential elections made a year in advance, such as the forecast of the 1938 congressional election, the 1940 and 1944 presidential elections, and the 1946 congressional elections; and among the short-range predictions, those based on the use of the formula: "As Maine goes, so goes the nation," and the various polls that became available during the course of a campaign.

The point I wish to emphasize in connection with these examples is that forecasts originate as appraisals of a political balance at a given time. They are then applied to some later date, on the assumption that certain developments are to be expected during the interval or that the situation will remain reasonably stable. If you must predict, this conception of a forecast will prove helpful. It provides a reliable excuse if the prediction goes wrong. In that case the forecast—you will rightly argue in self-defense—was merely an appraisal of an earlier situation; with conditions changed in the meantime, you expect your friends to forget it.

But if what you offer as an appraisal is subsequently borne out by the election results, you will, without too much protest, allow your friends to credit you with having made a good forecast. They will do so in spite of your protests.

Predicting elections is about as difficult or easy as predicting the course of business activity, employment, the stock market, or the commodity markets. Regardless of the successful experience of others, I prefer to regard predictions in these fields as an art and not a science.

There are four steps in the practice of this art: first, marshal the historical facts to discover the general trend or tendency, if any; second, ascertain the major factors that have caused variations in the trend; third, appraise the factors that are responsible for the current or latest development; and fourth, decide which factors are most likely to prevail in the future and estimate their possible effect. If no new elements appear other than those known to have prevailed in the past, one may forecast election results with confidence, and quite often with gratifying accuracy. There is always something new in politics, however, new faces and new issues, and their influence cannot be determined from a record, but must be inferred on the basis of one's general knowledge and experience. For this reason political forecasts are often based merely on past experience and are always a more or less hazardous undertaking.

Predicting elections, like predicting the business cycle or the stock and commodity markets, is sometimes considered a useless effort. With this view I am inclined to agree in part, if it is limited to election predictions so often made during the last phase of a political campaign, when practically nothing can be done by the contestants to alter matters. There is considerable evidence that voters' minds are pretty well made up long before election day. In such cases it would seem that predictions are of chief interest only to people who bet on elections.

Yet it is conceivable that even last-minute predictions could be of vital use to contestants and their parties. For example, Charles Evans Hughes is generally credited with having lost the 1916 election by an unusually narrow margin because he failed to carry California. Had he realized shortly before the election how close to defeat he was, he undoubtedly would have gone out of his way to shake hands with California's Senator Hiram Johnson and with that simple gesture have avoided the impression of snubbing the popular leader of the Western Progressives. Furthermore, on another occasion he would have avoided appearing in a photograph "on top of the San Francisco *Times* building ostensibly surrounded by notorious stand-patters in the strongly Progressive state of California." According to Professor W. E. Binkley's account in *American Political Parties*, the Democratic Committee saw to it that this "fatal picture" was given wide publicity. Hughes could have carried California—and become president—had he succeeded in winning just 1,887 more voters (0.4 per cent). Countless such hairbreadth defeats in our political history might have been converted into victories had last-minute predictions stimulated a final effort.

I would argue also, perhaps with particular emphasis, for the usefulness of election appraisals and forecasts made well in advance of the campaign, even in advance of the party conventions and the nomination of candidates. A forecast of the most likely outcome of an election is as valid in long-range political plans and operations as are long-range appraisals of the most likely course of the business cycle. In the case of an impending speculative boom or depression there is general interest in adopting plans for restraining the upward advance in prices and living costs, or checking the downward course of wages, profits, and job opportunities. Similarly, an impending shift in the political tide calls the major parties into action either to check or to hasten the turn of events.

Somebody must predict elections as well as the course of business. Congress has recognized this latter necessity in providing the President with a Council of Economic Advisers, whose job it is to analyze foreseeable trends in production, prices, income, and employment. If unfavorable business developments are in prospect, the Council must offer plans that would in effect alter the prospect and thus make their predictions go wrong. Likewise, if a pre-election trend is unfavorable to a political party, plans are made to check the decline. It is not sufficient to argue that many candidates have managers who constantly appraise their chances. Millions of voters, and particularly independent voters, could use their power more effectively if they too could appraise the course of a campaign.

Election appraisals and predictions will inevitably be made by both parties, and since they are likely to result in important decisions, objective analyses of basic facts are essential. For political as for business analyses we seldom have all the information we need. To predict the general course of business a year in advance requires data useful for predicting many factors in the business cycle. Likewise, to forecast a political election that will be held months or years later calls for forecasting the trends in domestic and international affairs.

We are, of course, discussing forecasts based on factual data—not on guesses, hopes, hunches, or clairvoyance—and since factual data refer only to the past and present, what we call forecasts are at best only analyses of the past, appraisals of the present, and projections of both into the future on certain assumptions.

As a rule we do not obtain forecasts from public-opinion polls; they are usually only appraisals of the present. Ordinarily people are not asked: "How are you going to vote next November?" but rather: "If you were voting today, for whom would you vote?" If nothing happens in the interval to alter the voters' judgment, and the election results check closely with the earlier poll, we call it a good forecast. If the election and the poll do not check, then something has happened in the intervening period and the poll was merely an appraisal.

In the last two months before a presidential election, almost anything can happen. The country can go into an economic tailspin, or some great international crisis may upset the political balance. If a business depression has not developed by September, however, it is most unlikely that a decline beginning in October will be severe enough to alter party prospects materially. International crises may come in September or October as well as any other time, and their timing or character cannot be predicted.

As a rule, only last-minue blunders or shrewd maneuvers on the part of the high command of either party can alter prospective results materially, and these, too, are not predictable.

Interpreting the Maine Election

The Maine election of September 15 always takes on nation-wide interest. Interpreted correctly, it could be of particular interest to campaign managers in planning their final efforts, not only in Maine but in New England and throughout the nation as well.

I have already indicated how the Republican victory in Maine in September 1936 enabled me to forecast a national Democratic victory in November. To emphasize the point that every appraisal and forecast has elements of certainty, uncertainty, assumptions, and guesses, I turn to rough notes jotted down immediately after the Maine election of September 1944. They show how current information, such as that obtained from polls, can be utilized to give the Maine election national meaning.

Notes on the Maine Election and the National Democratic Trend, September 1944 (Dated September 16)

1. Facts concerning the Maine election in September:
   (a) The state went 29 per cent Democratic, the lowest in many years.
   (b) The turnout was about 60 per cent of the vote cast in 1936–40.
   (c) A larger turnout, judging from the past record, would have meant a larger Democratic percentage.
2. Relation of the September gubernatorial and congressional vote in November:
   (a) A substantially larger turnout and a better Democratic showing in Maine is possible in November. In 1928, 1932, and 1940 the vote in November exceeded the vote in September by 48,000, 58,000 and 65,000 respectively.
   (b) The Gallup poll predicted accurately the 29 per cent Democratic vote for governor, and at the same time found Maine 46 per cent for Roosevelt.

3. Relation of the Maine elections to the national:
   (a) The margin of the Maine Democratic percentages in September and November to the national Democratic percentage has been a changing one.
   (b) Allowing for these changes, the national Democratic percentage in November may exceed the 29 per cent gubernatorial vote by as much as 23 to 25 points, indicating a national Democratic percentage of 52 to 54.
   (c) The Gallup poll, showing Maine 46 per cent for Roosevelt, and the relation of the Maine vote to the national as in 1940 mean a national Democratic percentage of at least 52.
   (d) This Democratic margin for the nation is being corroborated by current trends toward Roosevelt in Michigan, Iowa, Nebraska, Idaho, and Washington, which should raise the next Gallup poll from 51 per cent Democratic in July-August to 52 or 53 per cent as of mid-September.
4. The number of Democratic electoral votes for a national popular Democratic vote of 52 to 53 per cent:
   (a) Normally a national Democratic percentage of only 52 per cent might yield a bare margin in excess of 266.
   (b) There is ample evidence that the regional shifts that prevailed in 1916 and 1940 will again prevail this year, with the result that the Eastern and Far Western states will be more Democratic than normal and the Central states less.
   (c) On the basis of (1) the normal relation of each state to a national Democratic vote of 52 to 53 per cent; and (2) the 1940 regional shifts, the most probable number of Democratic electoral votes is between 276 and 339 and nearer the latter figure.
5. The normal line-up by states for a 53 per cent national Democratic vote, allowing for the 1940 regional shift: the "sure" Democratic states total 223 electoral votes; the "doubtful" Democratic states 116; the "doubtful" Republican states 109; and the "sure" Republican states 83.
6. Among the "doubtful" Democratic states (50–1 per cent) are Missouri, Ohio, Pennsylvania, and Massachusetts, with a total of 91 electoral votes. Among the "doubtful" Republican states (49–50 per cent) are New York, New Jersey, and Illinois, also with a total of 91 electoral votes.
7. Boiled down to a microscopic summary, this analysis seems to say that if Pennsylvania goes Democratic, Roosevelt can win even without New York.
8. The foregoing analysis of the mid-September Democratic-Republican balance makes no allowance for (a) the soldier vote; (b) the fact that the *Fortune* poll is now showing the nation 56 per cent Democratic; or (c) the common impression that victory over Germany might favor Dewey.

Predicting the 1938 Congressional and
1940 Presidential Elections

My experiences in predicting the 1938 congressional and presidential elections nearly a year in advance illustrate the range of assumptions I had to make, including a forecast of business conditions, international affairs, and the long-time political trend.

Early in 1938, after one of the sharpest recessions in business this country ever experienced in the course of one year, there was lively speculation about its effect on the congressional elections in November. This led me to examine the record of changes in business activity and party position in the House. I found that a 10 per cent decline in the business index tended, on the average, to be accompanied by a 10 per cent drop in major-party membership in Congress.

In order to utilize this formula early in 1938 in judging the outcome in November, it was necessary to project the business cycle for the intervening months. An estimate of the probable level of business for November 1938 was made on the basis of the typical behavior of earlier depressions. These suggested an upturn after the spring of 1938—a projection which seemed justified in view of the administration's reversal of its 1936–7 economy program. The level of business I then projected for October 1938 indicated that Democratic membership in Congress would be reduced from 77 per cent of the total to 60–5 per cent. The actual figure was 60 per cent.

After the congressional elections of 1938 it was logical to develop a basis for predicting the congressional elections of 1940. By the end of 1938 business was on the upgrade, and while there were differences of opinion as to its exact course in 1939 and 1940, it was generally agreed that whatever the intervening fluctuations, the business index would reach a higher level in the fall of 1940 than two years previously. With this assumption, it was natural to wonder what the Democrats or Republicans could expect in the 1940 congressional and presidential elections.

A partial examination in 1938 of the relations of changes in business activity to party position in Congress did not disclose that a rise in business improved the position of the dominant party after a business recession had caused it to lose membership.

It seemed to corroborate the generally held notion (which now needs to be qualified in the light of the facts in Chapter 6) that business depressions are more effective in taking parties out of power than business recoveries are in putting parties into power.

When a party in power begins to lose strength, as the Democrats did in 1938, was it likely to continue to decline in the 1940 and subsequent elections? The record was not too consistent on this point, but appeared to suggest that a further loss in House membership would not be an unreasonable expectation.

Business prospects for 1940 could not be predicted accurately; nevertheless, it was possible to project the underlying trend. The most reasonable projection that seemed possible in 1939, taking into account the possibility of war in Europe and the relief measures that might be adopted by Congress to curb unemployment, was that business activity would continue to improve well into the spring of 1940, and that, even with some decline, the average level would still be higher in November 1940 than in November 1938. In other words, it was possible to rule out a major business depression as a political factor in 1940 and to assume that there would not be a major third party. I also assumed that the United States would not be an active participant in a European war in 1940.

By this process of elimination I predicted that the political tide, as measured by congressional membership, would continue to run against the Democrats and they would suffer a very moderate loss of seats, from 61 to 58 per cent.

This tentative prediction of the political tide two years in advance was projected into the presidential race. As in every long-range projection, a number of imponderables had to be set aside and the forecast could only be attempted in general terms, ignoring the appeal of specific personalities. Assuming that Republicans and Democrats would nominate their best vote-getters, we predicted that if the Democrats won 58 per cent of the seats in the lower house, their presidential candidate would poll 54–5 per cent of the popular vote.

This, as it happened, proved to be an unusually good "forecast," but in studying subsequent events I was reminded of the frequent criticism that forecasts may be right for the wrong reasons. It applies in part to this case. Business did expand between 1938 and 1940, but our concern with the European war had much greater influence on the election by November 1940 than was assumed in 1939. The congressional index of the political tide, a key factor in my "forecast" of the 54–5 popular vote for 1940, did not as a matter of fact drop to 58 as assumed, but opposition to the third term for Roosevelt and the appearance of other minor issues that I had no way of anticipating in 1939 helped to produce the predicted presidential results. It should be observed that during the first six months of 1940, local elections and public-opinion polls corroborated the reasonableness of the forecast that 54–5 per cent of the 1940 popular vote would go to the Democrats.

"As Kelly Goes, So Goes the Nation"

The earliest clue to the possible outcome of the 1944 presidential election was contained in the Chicago mayoralty contest of April 1943, a year and a half before the national election. A brief discussion of it is included here not as an example of a foolproof method of long-range prediction but as an amusing illustration of the consistencies that abound in the voting behavior of the American citizen.

"As Kelly goes, so goes the nation," has been one of my private and fairly reliable long-range gauges of the New Deal political tide in presidential years. It has given "tips" eighteen months in advance as to the national Democratic-Republican balance. The younger generation of voters, coming of voting age in 1948 and subsequent election years, are likely to ask: "Who is Kelly and what is he?" Kelly was three times (in 1935, 1939, and 1943) elected mayor of Chicago, the second largest city in the United States and a fair political sample of the nation's population. He was preceded by Cermak in 1931, by Thompson in 1927, and succeeded by Kennelly in April 1947. Each of these mayoralty elections in Chicago hinted at the outcome of the national presidential elections in November of the following year.

In 1927 the Democratic candidate for mayor of Chicago received only 45 per cent of the votes; the next year Alfred Smith received only 42 per cent of the votes for president. In 1931 Cermak, a Democrat, was elected with 59 per cent of the Chicago votes; Roosevelt in 1932 received 57 per cent of the national vote. In 1935 Kelly came in on a landslide, polling over 80 per cent of the vote; Roosevelt in 1936 was re-elected on a presidential landslide with 62 per cent of the vote. In 1939 Kelly lost ground, only 56 per cent of the voters supporting him; Roosevelt in 1940 also lost ground, but won with a 55 per cent vote. In 1943 Kelly's popular majority fell to less than 200,000 compared with about 600,000 in 1939, and this was hailed as a sure sign that the Republicans would be swept into Washington the next year. Kelly, however, still held 54 per cent of the votes; Roosevelt in 1944 lost ground again, but he too won his third term with a 54 per cent vote. Finally in 1947 Kennelly replaced Kelly on the Democratic ticket and obtained 59 per cent of the votes. This was an unexpected reversal of the downward Democratic trend, interpreted by Republicans as a tribute to the appeal of a popular business and political figure.

Never having heard the formula "As Kelly goes, so goes the nation," the Democrats failed to recognize the full significance of Kennelly's election. Chicago again was symptomatic of the national trend, for by the spring of 1947 the Democratic fortunes had already risen from the low level of the 1946 congressional election. National polls on President Truman's popularity and the two-party preference in the spring, summer, and fall of 1947 showed an undeniable return of Democratic strength equal to or exceeding that of 1944 and 1940. On the basis of these developments, the stage appeared solidly set for a Democratic victory in 1948, until Henry Wallace's announcement on December 29, 1947 that he would seek the presidency on a third-party ticket and until other domestic and international complications (referred to in the last chapter) set in.

My notes contain this record on the Chicago mayoralty election, dated April 8, 1947:

"The figures (below) illustrate the political formula that 'As Kelly goes, so goes the nation,' which I now want to amend to 'As Kennelly goes, so goes the nation.' The following figures represent the percentage of the popular vote received by the Democratic candidates for mayor in Chicago for the past six elections and the corresponding percentages of the national popular vote received by the presidential candidate in the elections the following year.

Chicago Mayoralty Election			*United States* Presidential Election		
YEAR	DEMOCRATIC CANDIDATE	PER CENT OF VOTE	YEAR	DEMOCRATIC CANDIDATE	PER CENT OF VOTE
1927	Thompson	46	1928	Al Smith	41
1931	Cermak	59	1932	Roosevelt	59
1935	Kelly	83	1936	Roosevelt	62
1939	Kelly	56	1940	Roosevelt	55
1943	Kelly	54	1944	Roosevelt	54
1947	Kennelly	59	1948	?	?

"In considering the blank space left for the year 1948, it is necessary to bear in mind that the reason why the Chicago percentages and the national percentages in the following year show a fairly close correspondence is that there was no major change in economic and political conditions in these 18-month intervals. Perhaps the one exception is the interval between the Chicago election in 1931 and the presidential election in 1932; but in that case the change was merely a deepening of the business depression which was already unusually severe in 1931. Political attitudes in 1932 may have already been set by the magnitude of the depression in 1931. The foregoing comparison thus has predictive meaning only if one were to assume that there will be no major economic or political developments during the next year and a half to alter the present political balance suggested by the Chicago election.

"It would probably be realistic to assume that the 59 per cent of the votes cast for Kennelly contains a substantial vote that might not be available to a Democratic presidential candidate in 1948. But, even if the margin he received were cut in two, it would still suggest a Democratic figure of 54–5 per cent similar to that of 1943."

The devices for predicting elections are many, but those based on historical relationships and past trends should be supplemented and brought up to date by later information which can now be obtained through the greatly extended practice of polling public opinion. The next chapter shows how to combine historical analyses, projections, and polls.

Chapter 13:

Why Polls Go Right and Wrong

Polls are a scientific device for obtaining a cross-section of public opinion at a given time. Such a cross-section makes it possible to bring historical trends up to date and to project them into the future. For the purpose of predicting elections polls increase enormously the utility of such political records as have been introduced in this book. In this chapter I shall try to clear away some of the mystery from public-opinion polls and at the same time indicate how they can be used in assessing the two-party political trend at the beginning of 1948 and after.

It is surprising to find that polls are still generally regarded as magical devices. The Federal government has been using them for at least eighty years. Since 1866 the Crop Reporting Service of the Department of Agriculture has made annual forecasts of national crop production and livestock numbers on the basis of information received from a mere handful of farmer crop correspondents scattered over the important producing areas. As a rule, the information supplied by, say, two or three out of every hundred farmers has given the Department a fairly good indication of whether—and by how much—the farmers intend to expand or contract their acreage, and what the total national production of various crops appears to be at crop-reporting time.

The basic principle of sampling relatively few individuals to discover what, on the average, a large group think, is now used frequently in commerce, industry, and government. Experience has shown over and over again that where it is not feasible to take an expensive, complete census of all persons in a community, state, or nation, the sampling of a relatively few representative individuals or families is sufficient. "As the few go, so go the many," is the basic principle in public-opinion polling.

Though polls may go wrong, it is not because of any defect in the underlying techniques. Correct techniques may, of course, be injudiciously used—or misused—and the history of polling is full of blunders as well as successes. For instance, the peak of the New Deal tide in 1936 coincided with an outstanding demonstration of both good and poor polling. It witnessed the unnecessary demise of the *Literary Digest* poll and the subsequent rise of the Gallup, Roper, Crosley, and other polls. The *Literary Digest* emphasized sampling in large numbers, getting responses from millions; the others are based on sampling in small numbers, getting responses from a few hundred or a few thousand. The fatal error made by the *Literary Digest* lay chiefly in the interpretation of sample data, in not recognizing that quantity is not a substitute for quality.

The *Digest* undertook in 1936, as in earlier elections, to poll the nation on prevailing reaction to Roosevelt and Landon. It mailed millions of cards to telephone subscribers in all the states, expecting the large number of returns to ensure the correct results. On September 26, 1936 it published the returns of over half a million "ballots" from 21 states. Landon seemed to lead in 13 states and Roosevelt in 8. Fifty-nine per cent of those who responded favored Landon. By October 24 the number of replies had quadrupled to over two million. Landon's margin was whittled down to 54 per cent and Roosevelt still trailed with a mere 40 per cent. Even when the sample was quadrupled, it gave the wrong answer to the *Literary Digest*, for in the November election Roosevelt received over 60 per cent of the votes, not 40 per cent.

When the *Literary Digest* published the results of its straw votes, the Gallup polls indicated that Roosevelt was slightly in the lead. Though Gallup underestimated Roosevelt's real strength, he was, of course, closer to the fact. The Gallup poll was based on a few thousand replies in contrast with the millions who participated in the *Literary Digest* poll. Gallup, however, recognized the relative importance of representative sampling and took cognizance of the various economic groups, their occupational and other characteristics that make for differences in voting behavior. The *Digest* did not. It completely overlooked the many millions of voters who are not telephone subscribers, but who constituted the main group supporting the New Deal.

Even though the *Digest* failed to obtain replies properly balanced as between economic classes and regions, its results could nevertheless have been converted into an accurate poll by the use of a simple arithmetical adjustment. For example, 19,600 ballots from Iowa were marked for Landon and 11,800 for Roosevelt; Roosevelt thus had 37 per cent of the two-party total. In 1932 these same voters, the *Digest* ballots showed, had been divided 44 per cent Democratic and 56 per cent Republican, but Iowa as a whole actually voted 59 per cent Democratic in 1932. Had the *Digest* added 15 points to the Democratic percentage— 37 plus 15—it would have arrived at the correct Roosevelt trend in that state. Iowa would thus have been placed in the Roosevelt column. Similar adjustments for the entire *Digest* poll might have proved its adequacy and prolonged its life.

It is interesting to observe that in the very issue of the *Literary Digest,* September 26, 1936, which hailed a Landon landslide on the basis of the first half-million ballots, a popular columnist accurately predicted the result, thus demonstrating that, even with the advent of scientific polling, the good old-fashioned method of judging elections by personal observation and intuitive analysis still has its place. Part of her comment is quoted below:

> It looks as though he [President Roosevelt] will be reelected. And I do not think it will be a purchased vote, purchased by the bounties of the Federal Government—nor will it be the fact that the country is recovering, that business is on the upswing. No one believes that this process would be retarded by the election of Mr. Landon—this election will be decided less by thought than by instinct. But instinct is telling a great many people that Mr. Landon stands for Government doing as little as possible; for trusting

to the free play of economic forces to get and keep this country stable and progressive; and that Mr. Roosevelt stands for Government setting objectives, giving direction, and actively doing something. [Dorothy Thompson, *New York Herald Tribune* Syndicate.]

A scientific discourse on the art of sampling is not required to appreciate some of the common characteristics of the voting population that polling must take into account. The regional patterns of political behavior that we examined in Chapter 7, and the different regional effects of important economic, religious, and nationality issues examined in Chapter 8, indicate clearly that a sample typical of the nation should not be drawn predominantly from one area. It must be broad enough to represent all parts of the country. A test of political opinion in the Democratic South or Republican New England would in itself hardly tell us much about the nation unless we adjusted the results to equate local with national opinion. Similarly, in view of the diverse elements found in the population of any community, an effective sample cannot be drawn predominantly from any single area or social and economic group. We have seen, for example, that nationality and economic groups not only vary greatly in party preferences, but sometimes shift their political allegiances abruptly. (See tables in Chapter 9.)

Voters of Russian, Polish, Italian, and Irish parentage topped all other nationality groups in their support of Roosevelt in 1936, while those of German descent voted generally as the average citizen did. But in 1940, when the nation moved toward the Republican side by 7 percentage points, the shift among Italian groups was 25 points; German, 16; Irish, 10; and Polish and Russian, only 4.

The various economic classes also present wide and changeable political preferences. In 1936 84 per cent of the persons on relief voted for Roosevelt compared with 42 per cent of people in the highest-income brackets. In a typical city of up-state New York the silk-stocking wards voted predominantly for Willkie, while the factory workers' wards supported Roosevelt. On a national basis, 48 per cent of the business and professional group in 1936 supported the Democratic Party, compared with 74 per cent of the manual workers. By 1944 the spread between these two groups had narrowed, but still amounted to a difference of 20 points.

Local polls to be most successful must represent all the elements in a community, geographic, economic, and cultural; national polls to be most accurate must embrace communities in each of the significant regions.

Much has already been written on the technical problems encountered in sampling public opinion. The science of sampling is young and its standards and methods are still in a state of flux. They require evaluating and checking. Some of the questions still to be answered by public-opinion experts are: Should the sample be selected at random or at purposefully staked-out places? Should interviewers be given quotas, a specific number of businessmen, farmers, workers, young and old people, Protestants, Catholics, and Jews, women, men? Should the interviewer poll practically everybody in a given area?

Shortly after the 1940 election the prestige of public-opinion polls slumped because an outstanding poll had given President Roosevelt on the day before the election a very small popular margin and practically no electoral margin, whereas he won handsomely with a 55 per cent popular vote and 85 per cent of the electoral votes.

A meeting of the Washington, D.C. Chapter of the American Statistical Association in December 1940 afforded an occasion to demonstrate with political examples the effectiveness of polling by regions with complete coverage in small sample areas. These illustrations grew out of a study of county elections in relation to the national pattern. I chose to present some of my findings by presenting the (hypothetical) Bean Poll, Inc., with due apologies to the better-known Roper, Gallup, and Crosley polling organizations.

The information concerning the hypothetical corporation was presented in approximately these words:

"The parent corporation, in the interest of low overhead, requires neither a large board of directors nor a large staff of interviewers. Each member of the small board of directors must be a competent observer of public and political opinion in his own locality. By requiring that the directors serve also as the field staff, costs can be kept to a minimum. In selecting the board membership a new technique is to be adopted known as the 'Presidential' technique; this requires that each member of the board must be a *living past or present presidential or vice-presi-*

dential candidate. In 1940, the year of organization, these specifications automatically limit the board to the following six persons of great and specialized competence:

> Franklin Delano Roosevelt, chairman
> Wendell Willkie, vice-chairman
> Henry A. Wallace
> Charles McNary
> Herbert Hoover
> John Garner

"Now, any statistically competent prospective stockholder can see at a glance the sampling significance of this scientifically selected staff. Since each of the six board or staff members is expected to poll his own county thoroughly, it is clear that the assembled results will automatically represent a true cross-section of the entire country and all its political elements. Roosevelt is to report for Dutchess County, his home county, New York; Willkie, Wallace, and McNary their home counties in Indiana, Iowa, and Oregon, respectively; together the reports will give an East-West cross-section. Inasmuch as this cross-country line lies somewhat to the North, the reports of the other two staff members, Hoover's for his adopted county in California, and Garner's for his county in Texas, will add the proper Southern statistical ballast.

"The success of this venture is guaranteed 100 per cent by the probable record of performance. Had the corporation operated in each of the presidential elections from 1896 to 1936, inclusive, then the composite, average report from the six presidential and barometric counties would have predicted the winning candidate in every election, and their average margin of error, 2.5 per cent, would compare very favorably with the average of the outstanding competitors in the polling field as shown in the table below.

"This is certainly a proud record of potential past performance. We can afford to disregard the effect of a slight international bias in 1916 and 1920, and merely note for later adjustment the suggestion of religious bias in 1928. But the 1940 results, with the staff operating in the same territories, have been even more satisfactory, and every stockholder in the corporation (whether betting on the election or not) should be well pleased with the management. This poll for the six counties averaged 54.4 per cent

Democratic and the national vote was an actual 55.0 per cent Democratic!

Presidential Elections
(Democratic Percentage of Two-Party Vote)

YEAR	SIX "PRESI-DENTIAL" COUNTIES	UNITED STATES	MARGIN
1916	54.1	51.7	+2.4
1920	40.0	36.1	+3.9
1924	34.3	34.8	− .5
1928	35.8	41.2	−5.4
1932	56.2	59.2	−2.4
1936	61.7	62.5	− .8

| Average | | 2.5 |

"Such success surely warrants an immediate expansion program. The parent corporation, therefore, will lay plans for a subsidiary that will operate with a similar small force but apply a still newer technique of sampling for which it has already secured all the necessary patent rights. This second technique is 'diagonalization,' as simple and automatic as the presidential technique applied by the parent organization. It calls for establishing field representatives in the four counties located in the extreme corners of the United States, Maine, Florida, Washington, and southern California. A fifth representative is to be located in that county where the two diagonal lines connecting the Maine-California and the Florida-Washington counties cross. Since this just happens to be a western Kansas county, a bit off center (geographically as well as Democratically), it seems advisable to add an offsetting county somewhat east of center. The corporation, with the technical aid of the Census Bureau, has already discovered the particular county in Indiana in which the center of the nation's population is located. This provides the desired six counties, well distributed from the standpoint of representing geographical differences in public opinion, North, South, East, West, and central.

"The success of this subsidiary (its name has yet to be approved) is also 100 per cent certain as demonstrated by the following table. Probings reveal that had polling operations been carried on in these six counties they would have accurately pre-

dicted the winning candidates in all the presidential elections
from 1896 to 1936, with a very small margin of error. We note
again a slightly stronger international sentiment in these counties
than elsewhere and a rather sharper anti-Catholic bias.

Presidential Elections
(Democratic Percentage of Two-Party Vote)

YEAR	SIX "DIAGONAL" COUNTIES	UNITED STATES	MARGIN
1916	54.8	51.7	+3.1
1920	35.8	36.1	− .3
1924	30.2	34.8	−4.6
1928	35.6	41.2	−5.6
1932	60.4	59.2	+1.2
1936	63.1	62.5	+ .6
Average			2.6

"The results for 1940 are in line with this very satisfactory
record. The average of the polls of these six counties gave 54.9
per cent of the vote to the Democrats, compared with the actual
55.0 per cent for the country as a whole.

"The future for these hypothetical corporations appears very
bright, especially since there were other variations of these scientific sampling techniques that make possible the formation of
additional subsidiaries. For obvious competitive reasons these
cannot yet be revealed, but a mere hint will serve to justify our
great optimism. Our scientific staff has recently come upon other
heretofore not recognized political and geographical correlations,
such as the 'Adams' correlation. If interviewers are automatically
placed in all counties named Adams throughout the United
States, their pollings—judging from past records—will also re-
produce the national presidential results with great accuracy. It
is thus possible to envision any number of new polling companies
operating in Adams, Franklin, and other founder-named counties
so located as to yield representative cross-sections of public
opinion. It is the corporation's hope to make each subsidiary an
independent competitive unit."

I trust that no one will confuse this light-vein presentation of a
particular method of polling with my respect and admiration for
the progress the science of polling has made in the 1930's and

1940's, and the great and extensive service it has rendered in government and in private activity.

The ultimate problem in polling, as in all sampling, is to know how closely the results from small samples correspond to the characteristics of the total population sampled. The pre-election state-wide polls of the middle 1930's claimed a margin of error of only 4 points, which meant that if a candidate was favored on the average by 70 per cent of those interviewed, he could expect to receive anywhere from 66 to 74 per cent of the votes of the entire state; but that if a candidate is favored by only 52 per cent of the sample with a margin of error of plus or minus 4, he would be highly uncertain of his chances, for while he might get as much as 56 per cent of the actual vote and win comfortably, he might on the other hand get only 48 per cent and lose. It would, as a matter of fact, be highly unreasonable to expect polls based on a few interviews to be accurate in situations where a few votes or theoretically even a single vote among hundreds of thousands can throw the election to one candidate or the other. We should not underestimate the real usefulness and reliability of polls because they do not cope with all the statistical peculiarities of electing public officials by a majority vote.

Experiments with polling techniques during the 1930's and 1940's reduced the margin of error in state elections from plus or minus 4 points to plus or minus 2 points. Some of the nation-wide polls have come even closer in indicating the national division between our two major parties. Institutes of Public Opinion now operating in a number of European countries have also accurately measured the relative strength of candidates even where several parties were involved.

An interesting example of polling in a three-cornered mayoralty race in New York City was reported by Elmo Roper in the spring 1946 issue of *Public Opinion Quarterly*. The representative sample consisted of interviews with 515 (0.00025 per cent) of the 2,000,000 individuals who took part in the election three months later. The following rounded figures show how closely the preference of the carefully selected handful indicated in August the elections results in November.

In a closer race the differences of + 3 and − 5 points would, of course, be more important than they are here. In this three-cornered race O'Dwyer's landslide was clearly and truly predicted.

	INTERVIEW AUGUST PER CENT	FINAL NOVEMBER PER CENT	DIFFERENCE
O'Dwyer	54	57	+3
Morris	26	21	−5
Goldstein	20	22	+2
	100	100	±3

If we combine the historical relationships shown in Chapter 9 with current polls, the usefulness of the latter can be greatly increased. Early in 1940 the American Institute of Public Opinion polled several states on the relative strength of the two major parties by asking how persons interviewed would vote if a presidential election were held at the time, and published the results first for a few key states. Using only these few state returns and applying to them the usual state-national margins, I was able to indicate that the nation was about 54 per cent Democratic. This accurately anticipated the national average subsequently reported by the institute. The several national polling organizations, from March to July, found the sentiment of the country fluctuating around 54–5 per cent Democratic. In July, at convention time, the Roper poll showed 52 per cent of the voters favored Roosevelt, the Gallup poll 51 per cent; but as the campaign progressed, the polls indicated that Roosevelt was gaining ground, and in the final polling he received 55 per cent of the popular vote. In other words, from a sample of the Gallup sample, combined with historical relationships, I not only reproduced the Gallup results for all states combined in the spring of 1940 but also anticipated the results of the election.

In the spring of 1944 I again utilized a few Gallup state polls released in advance of the complete survey to anticipate both the national average at the time and the final election results. In April I concluded that the nation was no longer 55 per cent Democratic as in 1940, but about 53 per cent Democratic. At a time when the outstanding Democratic politicians were advising Roosevelt that he could not expect to win unless he dropped Vice President

Henry Wallace from the ticket, my notes indicate that I was inter-
preting the Gallup poll to mean that he would gain 53 per cent
of the vote regardless of his running mate. This was corroborated
by the Roper polls. My note concluded that "if a 53 per cent
popular vote is assumed, 35 states would go Democratic with a
total electoral vote of at least 400." The final result was 53.8 per
cent and 432 electoral votes for Roosevelt.

These two experiences in the early part of 1940 and 1944 are
interesting not only because the historical relationships and the
polls corroborated each other, but because they suggest a remarkable stability in public opinion with regard to the two major
parties. There was surprisingly little difference between the
indications at the beginning of each election year—before the
presidential candidates had been chosen and campaign issues and
slogans crystallized—and the final results.

What preview of the 1948 election results could be obtained
from the polls and the historical data at the beginning of that
year? During the last part of 1947 both the Gallup and Roper
polls showed that 55 to 60 per cent of persons interviewed thought
President Truman was doing a good job, compared with only 32
per cent who thought so in October 1946. About 54–5 per cent of
those interviewed stated that they would vote for the Democratic
presidential candidate if an election were held then. At the turn
of the year, polls in six Eastern states corroborated the fact that
the nation appeared to be divided 54 per cent Democratic and 46
per cent Republican, as in 1944.

The six states, as contained in the Gallup release for January 3,
1948, stood as follows on the question of party preference:

	PER CENT DEMOCRATIC
New York	53
Pennsylvania	51
Ohio	51
Illinois	51
Michigan	47
California	53
Average	51

If these six important states are on the average 51 per cent
Democratic, what is the most likely comparable figure for the

United States? The only way we can answer this question is to
assume that the relation between the six states and the nation
in 1948 is analogous to that in previous presidential elections.
We therefore compute for the elections from 1932 to 1944 the
average Democratic percentage for the six barometric states and
compare it with the national averages for the same elections, as
follows:

	SIX STATES PER CENT DEMOCRATIC	UNITED STATES PER CENT DEMOCRATIC	DIFFERENCE
1928	37.4	41.2	+3.8
1932	54.5	59.1	+4.6
1936	60.9	62.2	+1.3
1940	52.8	55.0	+2.2
1944	52.1	53.8	+1.7
1948 (January)	51.1	(53.8)	+2.7 (average)

These six states fell short of the national Democratic strength
by about 4 points in 1928 and 1932, and 2 points in 1940 and 1944,
an average difference of 2.7 points. Adding this difference to the
51.1 per cent average suggests that at the beginning of 1948 the
nation would give 53.8 per cent of its votes to the Democrats in
a two-party race—a figure equal to that of 1944. In 1944 a 53.8
per cent popular vote brought Roosevelt 432 electoral votes.
Normally, without the wartime influence on the electoral votes,
this proportion of the popular vote would bring the Democratic
candidate 352 electoral votes without New York and 399 including New York.

From these polls and the development of the historical relationship between the nation and states, we are led to conclude
that the Democratic Party at the beginning of 1948, as far as
popular opinion was concerned, had recovered from its setback
in 1946 and had an excellent chance—without taking into account
the possible effect of the third-party movement—to win the election, and, as shown in the next and final chapter, to start on the
first phase of a new and predominantly Democratic tide of the
1950's.

That chance however soon began to evaporate as the political
pot began to boil with a vigor unlike that of 1944, 1940, or 1936.
Following the threat to the Democratic prospects created by the

third-party movement, Democratic chances with Truman as a candidate for 1948 took a nosedive as one political issue was heaped upon another in quick succession. The extent of the deterioration is indicated in the next chapter. The relation of this abrupt change in Democratic prospects early in 1948 to this chapter on the use of polls in relation to historical political analyses is this: while historical analyses of political trends and relationships and political polls have their many uses, neither separately nor in combination can they reveal the outcome of an election early in an election year when much depends on the candidates to be selected and on the net effect of the powerful issues that have reared their heads before the election campaigns are set in motion. It is after the conventions have chosen the candidates that the combination of political history and opinion polls find their greatest usefulness in predicting the outcome of elections.

Chapter 14:

1948 and the Incoming Tide

The reader has been promised a summary of the major influences affecting the political tide since 1946 and a long-range projection of the political tide beyond 1948. The developments of 1947 are not difficult to review briefly, but to anticipate the outcome of the 1948 election and the future trend is obviously a venturesome and hazardous undertaking. One doesn't need to stick one's statistical neck out, but there isn't much fun in figures unless we can ride them into the future.

The evidence is clear that the year 1947 will go down in our political history as marking the end of the downward trend of the New Deal tide and the beginning of a new one. What kind of tide would be initiated with the 1948 election, and what course it would take during the decade of the 1950's can only be tentatively suggested by the sketch of a typical two-party tide drawn from the past.

Historians, like Professor A. M. Schlesinger, Sr., of Harvard, read the political record and projected the tide in terms of liberalism and conservatism, promising us the latter as the probable trend of the immediate future. On the other hand, I project the political tide more specifically in terms of a two-party balance, which does not necessarily imply that conservatism will dominate the 1950's. That balance will be determined by the success or failure attending the efforts of the party in power, Republican or Democratic, to smooth out the business cycle without creating unemployment and to establish peace. Should a strong third-party movement develop in 1948 and after, our history suggests that its most probable effect would be to revitalize the political alliances of the early 1930's that were weakened during the last half of the New Deal period and fell apart in 1947–8.

My summary of developments in the first year following Republican return to power in Congress will indicate why I conclude that 1946–7 may mark a turning point. To begin with, numerous signs at the end of 1947 pointed to another presidential term for the Democrats, the fifth in succession since 1928. The popularity of President Truman had risen sharply from the low point to which it had fallen in 1946. Independent voters, whose failure to go to the polls in 1946 helped to restore control of both houses of Congress to the Republicans, showed at the beginning of 1948 considerably greater preference for the Democrats than for the Republicans. The crisis in prices had not been solved. One of the major political questions of the day: "Whom will the voters blame for the postwar rise in prices and living costs?" was being answered in opinion polls and local elections. The Republican Congress was apparently blamed more than the Democratic President. The term "communism," with which Democratic candidates were unjustly labeled in the 1946 congressional elections, particularly in Catholic communities, was being applied instead in 1948 to a convenient new scapegoat, the third-party movement.

Business conditions in 1947 were good; production, employment, and profits high. This did not mean that many voters were not bothered by bread-and-butter problems. Nearly three fourths of them, according to the polls, found it more difficult to balance their personal and family budgets in January 1948 than in January 1947. Fifty-eight per cent of the farmers, who as a class were generally assumed to have fared unusually well under war and postwar high agricultural prices, indicated greater difficulty in meeting their bills in 1947 than in 1944. Labor unions complained that the Taft-Hartley Act had deprived them of the equality in bargaining with management that they enjoyed under the New Deal Wagner Act, and announced plans to raise funds for political action against 200 Congressmen who had voted for the Taft-Hartley bill.

There could be no doubt that the Republicans in 1947 had failed to hold the gains made in 1946. Practically all the special congressional elections during the year, and state and municipal elections in November as well, signified a Democratic revival. For example, in the Second Congressional District in Wisconsin only 36 per cent of the two-party vote went to the Democratic candidate in 1946, but in a special election in 1947 he received 49 per cent. The Democrat lost by a small margin, but his party had improved its position by 13 per cent of the total vote in one year. Another is the special election in the Third District of Washington in 1947. Although the Democratic candidate, ex-Congressman Savage, lost by 1 per cent, his party had gained 3 percentage points since 1946 and 6 points since the 1942 elections. His defeat was erroneously attributed to the charge of communism leveled against him and also against Henry Wallace, who campaigned in his behalf. A more likely reason was the failure of the Democratic organization to get out the vote: only 63,000 votes contrasted with 111,000 in 1944. The 1947 turnout was about as small as in 1942; more nearly normal participation would have elected the Democratic candidate.

The 1947 Democratic revival was evident even in city elections. In Indiana, of about one hundred cities more than half elected Democratic mayors in 1947 compared with only a fourth in 1937 and 1942. In Pennsylvania more than half of a selected list of thirty-one cities elected Democratic mayors in 1947, only about a fourth in the previous two elections. These special congressional and city elections and the public-opinion polls all told the same, and to most people surprising, story that had a presidential election been held at the beginning of 1948 the Democratic candidate, in a straight two-party contest, would have won with about as large a popular margin as Roosevelt's in 1940 and 1944. According to one national poll, the Democratic candidate would have obtained 52 per cent of the votes of white-collar workers, 58 per cent of the farmers, 61 per cent of the manual workers, and 43 per cent of the business and professional group in this hypothetical election. Except for a 10-point increase among farmers, who, on the average, had benefited from unusually high prices and earnings during the war and postwar years, had paid off a large part of their prewar indebtedness and accumulated considerable savings, this line-up would have resembled closely that of 1944, indicating a considerable gain over the Democratic position at the end of 1946.

The evident decline in Republican strength raised considerable doubt whether the prophecy that the party that loses control of Congress in mid-term elections is doomed to defeat in the next presidential campaign would be fulfilled. This prophecy is typically expressed by Professor Arthur N. Holcombe in his article: "The Changing Outlook for a Realignment of Parties," (*Public Opinion Quarterly,* Winter 1946-7):

> The effect of the mid-term congressional elections upon the prospects of the party in power in Washington has long been a favorite topic of political speculation. For many years the rule has been that the opposition party gains a substantial number of seats from the majority party. In modern times the only exception to this rule has been the election of 1934, when the New Dealers actually strengthened their position both in the Senate and in the House of Representatives. Generally the reaction against the party in power has not gone far enough to deprive it of the control of either branch of the Congress. Whenever such control has been lost, the following presidential election, since the disputed election of 1876, has invariably been won by the opposition. Thus the party in power lost the House of Representatives in the elections of 1930, 1918, 1910, 1894, 1890 and 1882, and lost the presidency in each of the following presidential elections. Naturally the loss of a mid-term congressional election has become an exceedingly bad omen for the party in power.

But the dominant reasons for the seven presidential victories by the opposition in the elections following those listed here involved business depressions in five cases and a third-party movement in another. My comment on this statement is therefore that as long as no depression and no third party were in the offing for 1948 the evidence of increased Democratic strength in 1947 appeared to be a bad omen for those who put their faith in the mid-term formula.

The 1948 presidential election promised to bring out a normal number of participants. Since 1920 only one presidential election

—that of 1944—has been marked by a subnormal turnout. The wartime reasons for that subnormal vote had largely disappeared in 1948. Fewer than a million and a half persons of voting age were in the armed services at the beginning of 1948, compared with over 10 million in 1944. Many war plants had been closed down or put on a peacetime basis, and war workers had either returned to their former communities or established themselves in new ones. Compared with 50 million votes cast in 1940, the normal vote for 1948, based on past participation and population increase, could reasonably be estimated at well above 55 million.

All these indications prior to the Democratic troubles of early 1948 nominating conventions could be taken as pointing to victory for the Democratic candidate in 1948, with a popular vote of 54 to 55 per cent—in a two-party contest. Such a vote could return the Democrats to power in the lower house, giving them about 55 per cent of the seats.

The remarkable recovery in Democratic popularity in 1947 was followed by an even more abrupt reversal in the first four months of 1948. The nosedive came in the three months after the third party revealed considerable strength in New York and other metropolitan centers. In that brief period there were concentrated also a number of politically potent developments. There was further deterioration in our relations with Russia as revealed by the President and the Secretary of State, and the President proposed legislation to increase military expenditures, to institute universal military training, and to again draft young men into the armed services. The President also sent a message to the Congress asking for legislation on civil liberties which aroused the South to talk of bolting the Democratic Party. The United States, having secured a United Nations decision to partition Palestine into two states, one Arab and one Jewish, reversed its position and thereby alienated not only Jewish voters in metropolitan areas and elsewhere but many others who saw in that reversal a severe blow to the United Nations.

For political forecasters a situation of this sort called for patience to allow the boiling political pot to quiet down to a normal pre-convention simmer.

The Gallup polls revealed the effects of this political turmoil in a decline in Truman's popularity in relation to possible Republican candidates. In Truman-Dewey-Wallace and Truman-Taft-Wallace polls in January, Truman outran both Dewey and Taft. In a similar poll in April, Truman outran only Taft and lost ground in relation to both Dewey and Taft. The third-party candidate in the Truman-Dewey-Wallace polls showed a slight gain from 6 to 7 per cent, and in the Truman-Taft-Wallace polls he gained two percentage points from 7 to 9. Of the combined Truman-Dewey sentiment, Truman had 53 per cent in January and only 45 per cent in April, and in the combined Truman-Taft sentiment, Truman had 62 per cent in January and only 54 per cent in April, a loss of 8 percentage points in three months.

By April 1948 it was common to hear that the Democratic Party was going to pieces. Democratic political leaders and other supporters of the Democratic Party in the South, in the large cities, and in various organizations were demanding a new Democratic candidate for 1948.

When so much is in flux statistical devices for short-range forecasts must be held in abeyance. It is wiser to lay out the long-range most probable political trend in the form of a typical political tide. From this we may judge whether the Democrats surmounted their 1948 pre-convention difficulties, or the Republicans capitalized on them sufficiently to counteract all the 1947 indications that their 1946 victory would be short-lived.

That the Republican victory in 1946 could be short-lived is suggested by my analysis of the course a typical political tide could take in the decade beginning with 1948.

In view of the irregular political record, what do we mean by a typical tide, and how does one project it into the future?

It is true that the record, as measured in chart 1 by Democratic membership in the House, does not represent a smooth or regular course. Throughout this book, in fact, I have emphasized the causes of some of the greatest irregularities. For the past hundred years there have been only three distinct alternating periods of power for each major party—hardly a sufficient basis, perhaps, for establishing the contours of a typical tide and projecting a normal long-time pattern. In spite of so many irregularities and so few cases, can we discover the characteristics of a typical political tide? We can get around the irregularities to some extent by the commonly used statistical device of averaging.

Let the reader examine once more the record in chart 1 and

note carefully the three Democratic peaks, 1856, 1899, and 1912, and the twenty-two-year periods after each of them, 1856–78, 1890–1912, and 1912–34. These are the three sections of the long-time record that I combine into one average or typical tide (table below). The results, in the form of a dual curve, the reader will find in chart 26. It merits close scrutiny. Note that I have placed the peak of the typical tide so that it corresponds with the year *1935*, the year in which (according to Chapter 3) the real peak of the New Deal tide occurred.

A Typical Political Tide
(Based on Democratic percentages of two-party membership in lower house)

PERIOD 1		PERIOD 2		PERIOD 3		
						AVERAGE OF
Year	Per cent	Year	Per cent	Year	Per cent	3 PERIODS
1856	59	1890	72	1912	70	67
1858	47	1892	64	1914	55	55
1860	28	1894	30	1916	49	36
1862	44	1896	39	1918	45	43
1864	24	1898	47	1920	31	34
1866	26	1900	44	1922	48	39
1868	30	1902	46	1924	43	40
1870	43	1904	35	1926	45	41
1872	30	1906	43	1928	38	37
1874	63	1908	44	1930	49	52
1876	53	1910	59	1932	73	62
1878	54	1912	70	1934	76	66
1880	46	1914	55	1936	79	60

What are the features of this average or typical tide? From a peak in 1935 it declines sharply for ten or eleven years (to about 1946); remains relatively unchanged for two congressional elections; then, about twenty-two years later (1956), rises sharply to another peak. It is rather amazing to find how closely the downward trend of the 1936–46 portion of the tide has paralleled the average of the three previous tides. It suggests a brief rather than a prolonged period of Republican dominance. It shows that the 1946 Republican gains were greater than normal for a mid-term election at the bottom of a Democratic tide and that the recovery in Democratic strength in 1947 is in line with the upper level of the typical tide beyond its (1946) mid-point.

This, the beginning of 1948, is about as far as we can travel with the record. Beyond this point the political tide may be charted in several directions.

The projected course of our typical tide is not so much a forecast as a stimulus to political speculation. It is not to be taken as anything more than one of several possible developments in the two-party or three-party fight for control of the 81st to 85th Congresses. *It is not a prediction of the shape of political things to come.*

The first point to observe before we begin on our own long-range speculations is that my analysis of the two-party tide and its projection is not the same as that of Professor Schlesinger's referred to in Chapter 2. Professor Schlesinger says:

> . . . energies greater than those residing in parties have swayed popular sentiment and bent Congresses and Presidents to their will. The nature and import of these energies become clearer if one forgets the much publicized role of presidential Administrations, masterful personalities, and political parties, and considers only the course of governmental policy as recorded in legislation and executive decrees. Certain trends immediately become manifest. Jefferson once observed that "Men, according to their constitutions, and the circumstances in which they are placed, differ honestly in opinion." One group, he said, "fear the people, and wish to transfer all power to the higher classes of society"; the other "consider the people as the safest depository of power in the last resort; they cherish them, therefore, and wish to leave in them all the power to the exercise of which they are competent." He called these contrasting attitudes Tory and Whig, aristocratic and democratic, Federalist and Republican. Today we should call them conservative and liberal.
>
> Any scrutiny of American political development discloses the alternate predominance of these opposing points of view. A period of concern for the rights of the few has been followed by one of concern for the wrongs of the many. Emphasis on the welfare of property has given way to emphasis on human welfare. An era of inaction—for stability generally suits the purposes of the conservatives—has usually been succeeded by one of rapid movement. Change in itself is, however, no index of purpose: the important thing is direction, whether it is towards less democracy or more.
>
> These swings of opinion can be plotted with reasonable definiteness. In some instances, historians might quarrel as to the exact terminal years, but at most such differences would involve only slight alterations. The analysis cannot be pushed back of 1765 because not until then did anything resembling national political movements exist in America.

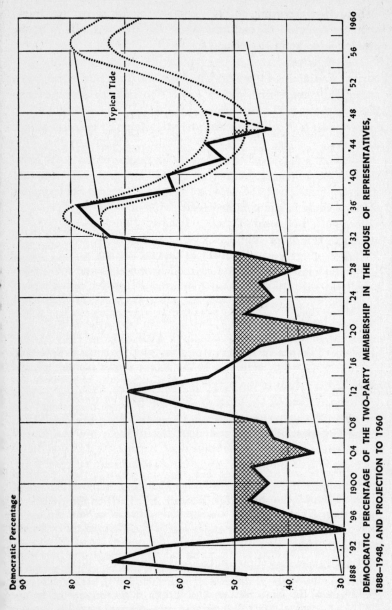

Democratic Percentage

CHART 26.

DEMOCRATIC PERCENTAGE OF THE TWO-PARTY MEMBERSHIP IN THE HOUSE OF REPRESENTATIVES,
1888–1948, AND PROJECTION TO 1960

The downward course of the New Deal tide, 1936 to 1946, paralleled the downward phase of an average or typical tide based on three previous tides (1856, 1890, and 1912). The typical tide points to Democratic congresses in the 1950's.

Thereafter, according to Professor Schlesinger, there were the following ten periods ending with 1931. The eleventh he predicted would end in 1947–8 and the twelfth in 1963.

Periods in American Politics

PERIODS OF LEFTWARD TRENDS	PERIODS OF RIGHTWARD TRENDS
1. 1765–87	2. 1787–1801
3. 1801–16	4. 1816–29
5. 1829–41	6. 1841–61
7. 1861–69	8. 1869–1901
9. 1901–18	10. 1918–31
11. 1931–47	12. 1947–63

The periods in the column on the left are called by Professor Schlesinger "Leftward Trends." I have, therefore, given the periods in the other column a comparable title.

The latest cycle of liberalism in this tabulation, 1931–47, approximates closely the period covered by what I have called the New Deal tide. But Professor Schlesinger's projection calls for this tide to be succeeded by a cycle of conservatism—a prediction that must be taken with caution. His tide for 1947–63 may not err materially in duration, but it could err greatly in character. While he predicts an era of conservatism, my studies suggest that the opposite is possible, that the 1950's might again see the dominance of liberalism in the national government.

What are some of the possible developments of the future that will affect the shape and character of the incoming political tide?

The first possibility, suggested by the records, is the election of a Democratic congress and president, but if a third party enters the field, one of the results might be a Democratic congress and a Republican president. Either of these possibilities could take place without either major party in the lower house having much more than 55 per cent of the membership. This would be no improvement over the near stalemate in the Congresses of 1942, 1944, and 1946.

What, in the meantime, might be happening to the price and business situation? Assuming no recession in 1948–9, but a continuation of high prices and great domestic and foreign demand for our goods, Congress undoubtedly will be called upon, as it was in 1947–8, to provide legislation for an orderly control and adjustment of a highly inflated price level.

Now suppose the third-party movement has gained strength as an almost evenly balanced Congress continues to withhold the necessary price legislation and authority for planning for the maintenance of full employment. In that situation, the congressional elections might return fewer Democrats to the 82nd Congress, partly because it will be a mid-term election (following our assumed Democratic gains in 1948), and partly because of the assumed third-party inroads. If the balance in Congress is thus further narrowed, the chances of legislative action proposed by either party to assure economic stability would be further reduced.

If in that impasse leaders in some of our basic industries assumed that the hour had come for the great postwar depression —that all the long and short so-called business cycles as popularized in 1947, the 54-year, the 18-year, the 9-year, the 3-year— were at last converging to produce a major depression in 1952, then we would see action. And if their fears actually fathered their actions and prices collapsed and unemployment mounted, the stalemate in the Congress of 1950 would give way to action as expeditious as in 1932.

The reader may set out a different sequence of political and economic events and he may wish to add assumptions with regard to international developments, which I have purposely refrained from doing. He may then wish to check his speculations with the second half of the typical tide projected from 1948 to 1960, which I present not as the political tide of the future, but as a reasonably likely one. If the actual course of Democratic strength in the lower house of Congress were to parallel the rising phase of the typical tide as it has the downward phase from 1936 to 1948, the Democrats—or their equivalents—will control more than 70 per cent of the seats in the lower house and dominate our political life during the last half of the 1950's.

Having thus laid out the shape and direction of the incoming tide, who will most likely sponsor it, and what shall we name it?

We are bound to hear more and more about the similarity between the political developments in 1948–56 and those of 1846–56, when the several varieties of Whigs and Abolitionists, and the Know-Knothing and Free Soil parties formed the Republican Party. Presumably the analogy will be used to suggest that out of the several liberal and progressive groups of 1948 will emerge a revamped party under the Democratic or some other name. If that is so, it has certain implications with regard to the support of labor, farm, and other organizations. Labor unions entered politics vigorously in 1924 in support of the LaFollette third party and reached, perhaps, the peak of political participation at the high point of the New Deal tide. Their preparations for 1948 and later campaigns are on a much larger scale than ever before. If labor and agricultural groups discover their mutual interest in a balanced relation between agricultural prices and wages, they might again support the Democratic Party or its 1950 model, as they did in the 1930's, and as they did a century ago when they endorsed the new Republican Party.

The most appropriate slogan of the dominant party in the next political tide, if history repeats, should bear some relation to the hopes and long-time aspirations of the majority of voters, particularly of the 1930's and 1940's. At the turn of this century, when labor was no longer welcomed in Republican councils, men made their way in political life with promises of a full dinner-pail but no promise that the dinner-pail would be full three hundred and sixty-five days of the year. Then came Theodore Roosevelt's Square Deal for business, labor, agriculture, and the professions. The next political era centered on Woodrow Wilson's New Freedom from trusts, monopolies, and the money power. After World War I, the brief interest in normalcy gave way to unwarranted faith in the continuation of the New Era of the 1920's. The inadequate measures for agricultural aid, labor's concern with evidences of technological unemployment, slow progress in social legislation, the free use of surplus profits in rigging the stock market, all brought on the great depression of the 1930's with its vast unemployment and its remedial political tide, the New Deal.

The New Deal era was concerned first with war on unemployment and then with war on foreign aggressors. Full employment was in part restored by the New Deal programs and in full by the war.

But in 1948 more than half of the nation—business, farmers, labor, and the professions—expected a business depression to develop in the immediate future and hoped their government would take the necessary action to prevent unemployment or mitigate its consequences. Many of the resource-development programs that were urged before the war and during 1946–8 are sure to be urged again if job opportunities become scarce. Whether the early 1950's mark a successful or unsuccessful national effort to maintain prosperity, full employment is bound to be our underlying concern for many years to come.

My final prediction then (which I do not expect any of my readers to check up on at least until 1956) is that the incoming political tide of the 1950's will mark the era of further progress toward the full use of our resources, and will be known as the Full Employment Era or by some other name expressing this general aspiration.

Statistical Appendix

TABLE 1: Numbers Voting as Per Cent of Total Population, Presidential Elections, 1888–1944

YEAR	TOTAL POPULATION (THOUSANDS)	TOTAL VOTE	PER CENT OF POPULATION
1888	60,496	11,381	18.8
1892	65,666	12,044	18.3
1896	70,885	13,813	19.5
1900	76,094	13,965	18.4
1904	82,165	13,524	16.5
1908	88,709	14,887	16.8
1912	95,331	15,031	15.8
1916	101,966	18,529	18.2
1920	106,466	26,705	25.1
1924	114,113	29,059	25.5
1928	120,501	36,879	30.6
1932	124,840	39,817	31.9
1936	128,053	45,647	35.6
1940	131,970	49,815	37.7
1944	138,083	48,026	34.8

SOURCE: *Statistical Abstract of the United States*, Bureau of the Census, 1946.

TABLE 2: Number of Eligible Voters and Votes Cast in 1940 Presidential Election, by States

STATE	NUMBER OF ELIGIBLE VOTERS [1]	NUMBER OF VOTES CAST FOR PRESIDENT	NUMBER OF VOTERS NOT PARTICIPATING	VOTES CAST AS PER CENT OF ELIGIBLE VOTERS
		(THOUSANDS)		
Total, U.S............	79,863	49,815	30,048	62.4
Alabama...............	1,555	294	1,261	18.9
Arizona...............	263	150	113	57.0
Arkansas..............	1,099	201	898	18.3
California.............	4,456	3,269	1,187	73.4
Colorado..............	688	549	139	79.7
Connecticut...........	1,012	782	230	77.2
Delaware..............	172	136	35	79.4
Florida...............	1,188	485	702	40.9
Georgia...............	1,769	313	1,456	17.7
Idaho.................	305	235	70	77.0
Illinois...............	5,120	4,218	902	82.4
Indiana...............	2,199	1,783	416	81.1
Iowa..................	1,609	1,215	393	75.5
Kansas................	1,145	860	285	75.1
Kentucky..............	1,631	970	661	59.5
Louisiana.............	1,365	372	993	26.0
Maine.................	494	321	173	65.0
Maryland..............	1,154	660	493	57.2
Massachusetts..........	2,575	2,027	548	78.7
Michigan..............	3,132	2,086	1,046	66.6
Minnesota.............	1,731	1,251	479	72.3
Mississippi............	1,195	176	1,019	14.7
Missouri..............	2,464	1,834	630	74.4
Montana...............	343	248	95	72.2
Nebraska..............	817	616	201	75.4
Nevada................	70	53	17	75.6
New Hampshire.........	296	235	60	79.6
New Jersey.............	2,593	1,973	620	76.1
New Mexico............	275	183	92	66.5
New York..............	8,328	6,302	2,026	75.7
North Carolina..........	1,925	823	1,103	42.7
North Dakota..........	358	281	77	78.4
Ohio..................	4,404	3,320	1,085	75.4
Oklahoma..............	1,362	826	536	60.6
Oregon................	717	481	236	67.1
Pennsylvania...........	6,031	4,088	1,943	67.8
Rhode Island..........	429	320	109	75.2
South Carolina.........	990	100	890	10.1
South Dakota...........	378	308	70	81.5
Tennessee..............	1,703	523	1,181	30.7
Texas.................	3,710	1,041	2,669	28.1
Utah..................	298	248	50	83.1
Vermont...............	214	143	71	66.8
Virginia...............	1,568	346	1,221	22.1
Washington............	1,124	794	330	70.6
West Virginia..........	1,046	868	178	83.0
Wisconsin.............	1,942	1,406	536	72.4
Wyoming..............	150	112	38	74.8

[1] Citizen population, native and naturalized, 21 years and over.

TABLE 3: Popular Vote for President, 1888–1944

YEAR	NUMBER OF VOTES CAST (THOUSANDS)			
	TOTAL	DEMOCRATIC	REPUBLICAN	OTHER
1888	11,381	5,540	5,444	397
1892	12,044	5,554	5,191	1,299
1896	13,813	6,468	7,036	309
1900	13,965	6,358	7,220	387
1904	13,524	5,084	7,629	811
1908	14,887	6,409	7,679	799
1912	15,031	6,286	3,484	5,261 [1]
1916	18,529	9,130	8,538	861
1920	26,705	9,147	16,152	1,406
1924	29,059	8,386	15,725	4,948 [2]
1928	36,879	15,016	21,392	471
1932	39,817	22,822	15,762	1,233
1936	45,647	27,477	16,680	1,490
1940	49,815	27,243	22,305	267
1944	48,026	25,603	22,006	417

[1] Includes 4,126,020 votes cast for Theodore Roosevelt.
[2] Includes 4,822,856 votes cast for Robert LaFollette, Sr.
SOURCE: *Statistical Abstract of the United States*, Bureau of the Census, 1946.

TABLE 4: Percentage of Total Vote Cast for Third Parties in 1912 and 1924 Presidential Elections, by States

	1912	1924
United States..............	27.4	16.6
Alabama..................	19.4	4.9
Arizona...................	34.3	23.3
Arkansas.................	17.5	9.5
California.................	41.8	33.1
Colorado.................	27.1	20.4
Connecticut..............	17.9	10.6
Delaware.................	18.2	5.5
Florida...................	8.7	7.9
Georgia..................	18.2	7.6
Idaho....................	24.1	36.5
Illinois...................	33.7	17.5
Indiana..................	24.7	5.6
Iowa.....................	32.9	28.0
Kansas...................	32.9	14.9
Kentucky.................	22.7	4.7
Louisiana................	11.8	3.3
Maine....................	37.4	5.9
Maryland.................	24.9	13.2
Massachusetts............	29.1	12.5
Michigan.................	39.2	10.5
Minnesota................	37.7	41.3
Mississippi...............	5.7	3.1
Missouri.................	17.8	6.4
Montana.................	28.1	37.8
Nebraska.................	29.1	23.0
Nevada...................	27.9	36.3
New Hampshire...........	20.2	5.5
New Jersey...............	33.5	10.0
New Mexico..............	16.9	8.5
New York................	24.6	14.3
North Carolina...........	28.6	1.4
North Dakota.............	29.8	45.2
Ohio.....................	22.2	17.8
Oklahoma................	...	7.8
Oregon...................	27.4	24.5
Pennsylvania.............	36.8	14.3
Rhode Island.............	21.7	3.6
South Carolina...........	2.6	1.2
South Dakota.............	50.2	37.0
Tennessee................	21.3	3.5
Texas....................	9.5	6.5
Utah.....................	21.6	20.8
Vermont..................	35.2	5.8
Virginia..................	15.9	4.6
Washington...............	35.3	35.8
West Virginia.............	29.9	6.3
Wisconsin................	15.6	54.0
Wyoming.................	21.8	31.5

TABLE 5: Presidential Elections, 1852–1944 (Per cent of Popular Vote cast for Democratic, Republican, and Other Candidates)

YEAR	DEMOCRATIC	REPUBLICAN	OTHER	DEMOCRATIC PER CENT OF TWO-PARTY VOTE
1852	51.0	44.0 [1]	5.0	53.7
1856	45.3	33.1	21.6	57.6
1860	29.4	39.9	30.7 [2]	42.4
1864	44.9	55.1	0	44.9
1868	47.2	52.7	.1	47.2
1872	43.9	55.6	.5	44.1
1876	50.9	48.0	1.1	51.5
1880	48.2	48.3	3.5	49.9
1884	48.9	48.3	2.8	50.3
1888	48.7	47.8	3.5	49.9
1892	46.1	43.1	10.8	51.8
1896	46.8	50.9	2.3	47.1
1900	45.5	51.7	2.8	46.8
1904	37.6	56.4	6.0	40.0
1908	43.1	51.6	5.3	45.5
1912	41.8	23.2	35.0 [3]	64.4
1916	49.3	46.1	4.6	51.7
1920	34.3	60.5	5.2	36.1
1924	28.9	54.1	17.0 [4]	34.8
1928	40.7	58.0	1.3	41.2
1932	57.3	39.6	3.1	59.1
1936	60.2	36.5	3.3	62.2
1940	54.7	44.8	.5	55.0
1944	53.3	45.8	.9	53.8

[1] Whig Party.
[2] Includes 18.1 per cent for Breckenridge; 12.6 for Bell.
[3] Includes 27.4 per cent for Theodore Roosevelt.
[4] Includes 16.6 per cent for LaFollette.
SOURCE: 1852–92 based on tabulation in Morison and Commager: *The Growth of the American Republic*, Vol. II, pp. 740–2. 1896–1944 based on tabulation from *Statistical Abstract of the United States*, Bureau of the Census, 1946.

TABLE 6: Democratic Percentage of Two-Party Presidential Vote, by States, 1896–1944

	1896	1900	1904	1908	1912	1916	1920
United States........	47.3	46.8	40.0	45.5	64.4	51.7	36.1
Alabama............	70.1	63.6	78.0	74.4	89.5	77.6	67.6
Arizona.............	...	...	...	...	77.6	61.8	44.4
Arkansas...........	72.9	64.5	57.5	60.7	73.8	70.4	59.7
California..........	45.6	43.1	30.3	37.3	98.6	50.2	26.8
Colorado...........	85.8	57.0	42.6	50.6	66.2	63.6	37.7
Connecticut.........	34.0	41.9	39.6	37.7	52.2	48.4	34.5
Delaware...........	44.3	45.6	44.9	46.9	58.5	48.8	43.1
Florida.............	73.1	79.1	76.5	74.5	89.5	79.3	66.9
Georgia............	61.2	70.3	77.6	63.6	93.8	91.9	71.2
Idaho..............	78.6	51.9	27.9	40.7	50.8	55.8	34.4
Illinois.............	43.3	45.7	34.1	41.7	61.5	45.2	27.3
Indiana............	48.6	48.0	42.7	49.2	65.1	49.5	42.3
Iowa...............	43.6	40.5	32.6	42.2	60.7	44.1	26.4
Kansas	51.9	46.3	28.8	45.0	65.7	53.2	33.4
Kentucky...........	50.0	50.9	51.4	50.9	65.5	52.7	50.2
Louisiana...........	80.8	79.0	90.2	87.7	94.0	92.5	69.4
Maine..............	30.1	36.3	29.7	34.6	65.8	47.9	30.2
Maryland...........	43.3	47.3	50.0	49.9	67.2	54.1	43.3
Massachusetts.......	27.5	39.7	39.1	36.9	52.8	48.0	28.9
Michigan...........	44.7	40.1	27.0	34.4	49.8	45.7	23.4
Minnesota..........	41.9	37.2	20.3	35.8	62.3	49.9	21.6
Mississippi.........	92.8	89.8	94.2	93.3	97.3	95.0	85.7
Missouri............	54.4	52.8	48.0	49.9	61.4	51.9	44.1
Montana...........	80.2	59.4	38.4	47.6	60.1	60.2	34.4
Nebraska...........	52.7	48.3	27.6	50.8	66.8	57.4	32.6
Nevada............	80.1	62.2	36.7	51.0	71.4	59.4	38.9
New Hampshire......	27.0	39.3	38.6	38.8	51.3	50.0	39.7
New Jersey..........	37.6	42.6	40.2	40.8	66.7	44.0	29.6
New Mexico.........	...	...	...	...	53.5	51.9	44.7
New York...........	40.2	45.2	44.3	43.4	59.0	46.6	29.4
North Carolina.......	53.1	54.2	60.1	54.4	83.2	58.2	56.7
North Dakota........	44.0	36.4	21.3	36.3	56.3	50.8	18.9
Ohio...............	47.6	46.6	36.5	46.8	60.4	54.0	39.8
Oklahoma...........	...	...	...	54.3	56.9	60.3	46.8
Oregon.............	48.9	41.8	22.5	37.8	57.6	48.6	35.8
Pennsylvania........	37.0	37.3	28.7	37.5	59.1	42.6	29.3
Rhode Island........	27.9	37.0	37.4	36.0	52.3	47.4	33.9
South Carolina.......	88.8	93.0	95.4	94.0	98.9	97.6	96.6
South Dakota........	50.1	42.0	23.4	37.3	100	48.0	24.5
Tennessee...........	52.4	54.1	55.5	53.5	68.7	56.8	48.5
Texas...............	64.0	67.1	76.8	76.1	88.5	81.6	71.5
Utah...............	82.7	48.8	34.9	41.1	46.5	60.8	41.0
Vermont............	16.6	23.2	19.5	22.5	39.7	36.1	23.5
Virginia............	53.4	55.8	62.6	61.2	79.5	67.6	61.8
Washington.........	56.9	43.8	21.7	35.5	55.2	52.3	27.4
West Virginia........	47.3	45.1	43.2	44.7	66.6	48.7	43.9
Wisconsin...........	38.2	37.5	30.7	40.2	55.7	46.4	18.5
Wyoming............	50.7	41.2	30.3	41.7	51.3	56.6	33.2

Continuation of: TABLE 6: Democratic Percentage of Two-Party Presidential Vote by States, 1896– 1944

	1924	1928	1932	1936	1940	1944
United States	34.8	41.2	59.1	62.2	55.0	53.8
Alabama	72.5	51.4	85.5	87.1	85.6	81.7
Arizona	46.2	42.3	68.7	72.2	63.8	59.0
Arkansas	67.6	61.3	87.3	82.1	79.0	70.1
California	12.6	34.6	61.0	67.9	58.3	56.8
Colorado	27.8	34.4	56.9	61.9	48.7	46.6
Connecticut	31.9	45.9	49.4	57.8	53.7	52.7
Delaware	38.6	33.9	48.8	56.3	54.8	54.6
Florida	67.0	41.4	74.9	76.1	74.0	70.3
Georgia	80.3	66.4	92.2	87.4	91.7	82.6
Idaho	25.8	34.8	60.6	65.5	54.5	51.8
Illinois	28.4	42.6	56.8	59.2	51.3	51.8
Indiana	41.2	39.9	56.0	57.5	49.2	47.1
Iowa	23.0	37.8	59.1	56.0	47.8	47.7
Kansas	27.7	27.3	54.9	53.9	42.7	39.4
Kentucky	48.6	40.6	59.5	59.4	57.6	54.7
Louisiana	79.1	76.3	93.0	88.8	85.9	80.6
Maine	23.3	31.1	43.6	42.8	48.8	47.5
Maryland	47.7	42.6	63.0	62.7	58.8	51.9
Massachusetts	28.5	50.5	52.1	55.1	53.4	52.9
Michigan	14.8	29.1	54.1	59.2	49.8	50.5
Minnesota	11.7	41.4	62.3	66.6	51.9	52.8
Mississippi	92.2	82.6	96.4	97.2	98.4	97.8
Missouri	47.0	44.3	64.5	61.4	52.4	51.5
Montana	31.3	40.9	62.0	71.5	59.4	54.7
Nebraska	38.5	36.4	64.1	58.4	42.8	41.4
Nevada	34.4	43.5	69.4	72.8	60.2	54.6
New Hampshire	36.7	41.2	49.3	50.9	53.2	52.1
New Jersey	30.6	40.0	51.0	60.1	51.8	50.7
New Mexico	47.0	40.9	63.5	63.2	56.7	53.6
New York	34.3	48.8	56.7	60.2	51.5	52.5
North Carolina	59.8	45.1	70.5	73.4	74.0	66.7
North Dakota	12.7	44.8	71.3	69.2	42.5	45.8
Ohio	28.9	34.7	51.5	60.8	52.2	49.8
Oklahoma	53.1	35.8	73.3	67.1	57.7	55.7
Oregon	32.2	34.7	61.1	68.5	54.1	52.5
Pennsylvania	22.6	34.4	47.1	58.2	53.5	51.4
Rhode Island	37.9	50.3	56.0	56.9	56.8	58.7
South Carolina	97.8	95.2	98.1	98.6	97.5	95.2
South Dakota	21.2	39.4	64.9	56.0	42.6	41.7
Tennessee	54.9	44.6	67.2	69.1	67.5	60.6
Texas	78.7	48.1	88.5	87.6	80.9	81.1
Utah	37.8	46.1	57.9	69.9	62.4	60.7
Vermont	16.7	33.0	41.6	43.4	45.0	42.9
Virginia	65.6	46.0	69.5	70.5	68.3	62.5
Washington	16.3	31.8	62.9	69.0	58.9	57.4
West Virginia	47.1	41.3	55.0	60.7	57.1	54.9
Wisconsin	17.9	45.3	67.0	67.8	51.8	49.1
Wyoming	23.5	35.7	57.9	61.8	53.0	48.8

TABLE 7: Democratic Percentage of Total Presidential Vote, by States, 1896–1944

	1896	1900	1904	1908	1912	1916	1920
United States........	45.9	45.5	37.6	43.1	41.9	49.3	34.1
Alabama............	67.0	60.8	73.3	70.7	69.9	76.0	66.7
Arizona.............	...	...	...	...	51.0	57.2	44.2
Arkansas...........	72.0	63.5	55.0	57.4	55.6	66.6	58.1
California.........	41.1	41.2	27.0	33.0	41.8	46.6	24.3
Colorado...........	85.0	55.5	41.1	48.0	42.9	60.7	35.9
Connecticut........	32.5	41.1	38.1	35.9	39.2	46.7	33.0
Delaware...........	42.6	44.9	44.1	46.0	46.4	47.8	42.1
Florida.............	66.0	71.0	68.8	63.0	70.1	69.3	58.1
Georgia............	59.7	66.9	64.3	54.9	77.7	80.0	71.2
Idaho..............	78.1	50.7	25.5	37.2	32.1	52.0	34.3
Illinois............	42.7	44.6	30.4	39.0	35.3	43.4	25.5
Indiana............	48.0	46.7	40.2	46.9	43.1	46.5	40.5
Iowa...............	43.0	39.5	30.7	40.6	37.6	42.9	25.4
Kansas.............	51.1	45.7	26.2	42.9	39.3	50.0	32.5
Kentucky...........	48.9	50.2	49.8	49.8	48.5	51.9	49.7
Louisiana..........	76.3	79.0	88.5	84.7	76.7	85.9	69.2
Maine..............	29.2	35.1	28.5	33.3	39.4	46.9	29.8
Maryland...........	41.7	46.2	48.8	48.6	48.6	52.8	42.2
Massachusetts.......	26.3	37.8	37.2	34.0	35.6	46.6	27.8
Michigan...........	43.5	38.9	25.8	32.4	27.4	43.9	22.3
Minnesota..........	40.9	35.7	18.8	33.1	31.8	46.2	19.4
Mississippi.........	91.0	87.6	91.1	90.3	88.8	93.3	84.0
Missouri...........	53.9	51.5	46.0	48.4	47.3	50.6	43.1
Montana...........	79.9	58.4	33.8	42.6	35.0	56.9	32.0
Nebraska...........	51.5	47.2	23.4	49.1	43.7	55.3	31.1
Nevada............	75.6	62.2	32.9	45.7	39.7	53.4	36.2
New Hampshire......	25.4	38.4	37.8	37.6	39.5	49.1	39.4
New Jersey.........	36.0	41.1	38.1	39.1	41.2	42.7	28.4
New Mexico.........	...	...	...	...	41.4	50.3	44.3
New York...........	38.7	43.8	42.3	40.7	41.3	44.5	26.9
North Carolina......	53.1	53.9	59.7	54.3	59.2	58.1	56.7
North Dakota........	44.0	35.5	21.3	34.8	34.2	47.8	18.9
Ohio...............	47.1	45.7	34.3	44.8	41.0	51.9	38.6
Oklahoma...........	...	...	...	49.8	47.1	50.6	44.5
Oregon.............	48.0	39.6	19.4	34.3	34.3	45.9	33.5
Pennsylvania........	35.8	36.2	27.3	35.3	32.5	40.2	27.2
Rhode Island........	26.4	35.0	36.2	34.2	39.0	46.0	32.8
South Carolina......	88.8	93.0	95.4	93.8	96.0	96.7	96.0
South Dakota........	49.7	41.1	21.7	35.1	41.8	45.9	19.7
Tennessee..........	51.5	53.0	54.2	52.7	52.6	56.2	48.3
Texas..............	53.9	63.4	71.7	73.2	72.7	77.0	59.2
Utah...............	82.7	48.4	32.9	39.2	32.6	58.8	38.8
Vermont............	15.9	22.9	18.8	21.8	24.4	35.2	23.2
Virginia............	52.6	55.3	61.6	60.5	66.0	66.8	61.3
Washington.........	55.2	41.7	19.4	31.8	27.0	48.1	21.1
West Virginia........	46.8	44.7	42.0	43.2	42.8	48.4	43.3
Wisconsin..........	37.0	36.0	28.0	36.7	41.1	42.8	16.2
Wyoming...........	49.2	41.2	29.1	41.7	36.2	54.6	31.9

Continuation of: TABLE 7: Democratic Percentage of Total Presidential Vote, by States, 1896–1944

	1924	1928	1932	1936	1940	1944
United States.........	28.8	40.8	57.4	60.2	54.7	53.3
Alabama.............	68.7	51.3	84.8	86.4	85.2	81.3
Arizona..............	35.5	42.2	67.0	69.9	63.5	58.8
Arkansas.............	61.2	60.3	86.0	81.8	78.6	70.0
California............	8.2	34.2	58.4	67.0	57.5	56.5
Colorado.............	22.0	34.0	54.8	60.4	48.4	46.4
Connecticut..........	27.5	45.6	47.4	55.3	53.4	52.3
Delaware............	36.4	34.6	48.1	54.6	54.7	54.4
Florida..............	56.9	40.1	74.7	76.1	74.0	70.3
Georgia.............	74.1	56.6	91.6	87.1	84.8	81.7
Idaho...............	16.4	34.4	58.7	63.0	54.4	51.6
Illinois..............	23.4	42.3	55.2	57.7	51.0	51.5
Indiana.............	38.7	39.6	54.7	56.6	49.0	46.7
Iowa................	16.5	37.5	57.7	54.4	47.6	47.5
Kansas..............	23.6	27.1	53.6	53.7	42.4	39.2
Kentucky............	46.1	40.5	59.0	58.5	57.4	54.5
Louisiana............	76.4	76.3	92.8	88.8	85.9	80.6
Maine...............	21.8	31.0	43.2	41.5	48.8	47.4
Maryland............	41.3	42.3	61.5	62.3	58.3	51.9
Massachusetts........	24.9	50.2	50.6	51.2	53.1	52.8
Michigan............	13.1	28.9	52.4	56.3	49.5	50.2
Minnesota...........	6.8	40.8	59.9	61.8	51.5	52.4
Mississippi...........	89.4	82.1	96.0	97.1	95.7	88.0
Missouri.............	43.9	44.1	63.7	60.8	52.3	51.4
Montana.............	19.4	40.5	58.8	69.3	58.8	54.3
Nebraska............	29.6	36.2	63.0	57.1	42.8	41.4
Nevada..............	21.9	43.5	69.4	72.8	60.2	54.6
New Hampshire.......	34.7	41.0	49.0	49.7	53.2	52.1
New Jersey...........	27.4	39.8	49.5	59.5	51.5	50.3
New Mexico..........	43.0	40.9	62.7	62.7	56.7	53.5
New York............	29.1	47.4	54.1	53.9	51.5 [1]	52.3 [1]
North Carolina.......	59.0	45.1	69.9	73.4	74.0	66.7
North Dakota........	7.0	44.5	69.6	59.6	44.5	45.5
Ohio................	23.7	34.5	49.9	58.0	52.2	49.8
Oklahoma............	48.5	35.4	73.3	66.8	57.4	55.6
Oregon..............	24.2	34.1	58.0	64.4	53.7	51.8
Pennsylvania.........	19.1	33.9	45.3	56.9	53.2	51.1
Rhode Island.........	36.5	50.2	55.1	53.1	56.7	58.6
South Carolina.......	96.6	91.4	98.0	98.6	95.6	87.6
South Dakota........	13.3	39.2	63.6	54.0	42.6	41.7
Tennessee............	52.9	46.0	66.5	68.8	67.3	60.4
Texas...............	73.6	48.1	88.1	87.1	80.7	71.4
Utah................	29.9	45.9	56.5	69.3	62.3	60.4
Vermont.............	15.7	32.9	41.1	43.2	44.9	42.9
Virginia.............	62.5	45.9	68.5	70.2	68.1	62.4
Washington..........	10.2	31.3	57.5	66.4	58.2	56.8
West Virginia........	44.1	41.0	54.5	60.5	57.1	54.9
Wisconsin............	8.1	44.3	63.5	63.8	50.1	48.6
Wyoming............	16.1	35.4	56.1	60.6	52.8	48.8

[1] Includes votes cast by American Labor and Liberal parties.

TABLE 8: State Democratic Percentages of Two-Party Presidential Vote Corresponding to National Democratic Percentages of 40 to 60

	40.0	45.0	48.0	49.0	50.0	51.0
United States	40.0	45.0	48.0	49.0	50.0	51.0
Alabama	73.0	76.3	78.2	78.9	79.5	80.1
Arizona	49.8	54.9	57.9	58.9	59.9	60.9
Arkansas	66.8	70.3	72.4	73.1	73.8	74.5
California	27.9	36.9	42.3	44.1	45.9	47.7
Colorado	37.7	43.2	46.5	47.6	48.7	49.8
Connecticut	36.9	41.5	44.4	45.4	46.3	47.2
Delaware	43.5	46.4	48.1	48.7	49.3	49.9
Florida	68.5	70.2	71.2	71.6	71.9	72.2
Georgia	77.7	79.9	81.2	81.6	82.0	82.5
Idaho	36.1	42.7	46.7	48.0	49.3	50.7
Illinois	33.6	39.0	42.5	43.7	44.8	46.0
Indiana	44.5	47.4	49.2	49.8	50.4	50.9
Iowa	30.0	35.8	39.3	40.5	41.7	42.8
Kansas	34.6	39.0	41.6	42.5	43.4	44.3
Kentucky	51.1	53.1	54.2	54.6	54.9	55.3
Louisiana	76.7	79.4	81.1	81.6	82.1	82.6
Maine	29.5	32.5	34.3	34.9	35.5	36.1
Maryland	48.4	51.6	53.5	54.2	54.8	55.4
Massachusetts	33.2	38.1	41.1	42.1	43.1	44.0
Michigan	25.9	33.4	37.9	39.4	40.9	42.4
Minnesota	25.1	34.5	40.1	42.0	43.9	45.7
Mississippi	90.4	91.9	92.8	93.1	93.4	93.8
Missouri	48.3	51.2	53.0	53.6	54.1	54.6
Montana	39.4	46.7	51.1	52.5	54.0	55.4
Nebraska	39.4	43.7	46.3	47.1	48.0	48.8
Nevada	42.8	49.5	53.6	54.9	56.3	57.6
New Hampshire	40.4	42.8	44.2	44.7	45.2	45.7
New Jersey	35.1	40.7	44.1	45.2	46.3	47.4
New Mexico	48.8	52.0	54.0	54.6	55.2	55.9
New York	36.3	41.2	44.1	45.1	46.1	47.1
North Carolina	60.9	63.7	65.4	66.0	66.6	67.1
North Dakota	24.8	34.8	40.8	42.8	44.8	46.8
Ohio	38.9	43.8	46.8	47.8	48.8	49.7
Oklahoma	52.9	56.1	58.1	58.7	59.3	59.9
Oregon	39.8	46.3	50.2	51.5	52.8	54.0
Pennsylvania	31.5	37.5	41.1	42.3	43.5	44.8
Rhode Island	39.4	43.3	45.6	46.4	47.2	48.0
South Carolina	97.8	98.0	98.1	98.1	98.1	98.2
South Dakota	28.5	34.7	38.4	39.7	40.9	42.1
Tennessee	54.6	57.8	59.7	60.3	61.0	61.6
Texas	77.3	79.7	81.1	81.6	82.0	82.5
Utah	44.5	50.2	53.6	54.8	55.9	57.0
Vermont	24.0	28.4	31.0	31.9	32.8	33.6
Virginia	64.9	65.9	66.7	66.9	67.2	67.5
Washington	29.8	38.6	43.9	45.6	47.4	49.2
West Virginia	48.1	50.9	52.6	53.2	53.9	54.3
Wisconsin	26.6	35.9	41.5	43.3	45.2	47.1
Wyoming	34.0	40.3	44.0	45.3	46.6	47.8

Continuation of: TABLE 8: State Democratic Percentages, etc.

	52.0	53.0	54.0	55.0	56.0	60.0
United States.........	52.0	53.0	54.0	55.0	56.0	60.0
Alabama..............	80.8	81.4	82.1	82.7	83.3	85.8
Arizona...............	61.9	62.9	63.9	64.9	65.9	70.0
Arkansas..............	75.2	75.9	76.6	77.3	78.0	80.6
California............	49.5	51.3	53.1	54.9	56.7	64.1
Colorado..............	50.9	52.0	53.1	54.2	55.2	59.5
Connecticut...........	48.2	49.1	50.1	51.1	52.0	55.7
Delaware.............	50.5	51.0	51.6	52.2	52.8	55.1
Florida...............	72.6	72.9	73.3	73.6	73.9	75.3
Georgia...............	82.9	83.3	83.8	84.2	84.6	86.3
Idaho.................	52.0	53.3	54.7	56.0	57.3	62.7
Illinois...............	47.2	48.4	49.5	50.7	51.9	57.0
Indiana...............	51.5	52.1	52.7	53.3	53.9	56.3
Iowa..................	44.0	45.2	46.3	47.5	48.7	53.4
Kansas...............	45.2	46.0	46.9	47.8	48.7	52.2
Kentucky.............	55.7	56.1	56.4	56.8	57.2	58.5
Louisiana.............	83.2	83.7	84.3	84.8	85.3	87.5
Maine................	36.7	37.3	37.9	38.5	39.1	41.5
Maryland.............	56.1	56.7	57.4	58.0	58.7	61.2
Massachusetts.........	45.0	46.0	47.0	48.0	49.0	53.0
Michigan.............	43.9	45.4	46.9	48.4	49.9	55.9
Minnesota............	47.6	49.5	51.3	53.2	55.1	62.5
Mississippi...........	94.1	94.4	94.7	95.0	95.3	96.6
Missouri..............	55.2	55.8	56.4	57.0	57.6	60.1
Montana..............	56.9	58.3	59.8	61.2	62.7	68.4
Nebraska.............	49.6	50.5	51.4	52.7	53.0	56.4
Nevada...............	59.0	60.3	61.7	63.0	64.4	69.8
New Hampshire........	46.2	46.6	47.1	47.6	48.1	50.0
New Jersey...........	48.5	49.7	50.8	51.9	53.0	57.5
New Mexico...........	56.5	57.1	57.7	58.3	59.0	61.4
New York.............	48.1	49.0	50.0	51.0	52.0	56.4
North Carolina........	67.7	68.3	68.8	69.4	70.0	72.3
North Dakota........	48.8	50.8	52.8	54.8	56.8	64.8
Ohio.................	50.7	51.7	52.7	53.7	54.7	58.7
Oklahoma............	60.6	61.2	61.9	62.5	63.1	65.7
Oregon...............	55.3	56.6	57.9	59.2	60.5	65.6
Pennsylvania..........	46.0	47.2	48.4	49.6	50.8	55.7
Rhode Island.........	48.8	49.5	50.3	51.1	51.9	55.0
South Carolina........	98.2	98.2	98.3	98.3	98.3	98.4
South Dakota..........	43.4	44.6	45.9	47.1	48.3	53.3
Tennessee.............	62.3	62.9	63.6	64.2	64.8	67.4
Texas.................	83.0	83.5	83.9	84.4	84.9	86.7
Utah.................	58.2	59.3	60.5	61.6	62.7	67.3
Vermont..............	34.5	35.4	36.3	37.1	38.0	41.4
Virginia...............	67.7	68.0	68.3	68.6	68.9	70.1
Washington...........	50.9	52.7	54.4	56.2	58.0	65.0
West Virginia.........	54.9	55.5	56.0	56.6	57.2	59.5
Wisconsin.............	48.9	50.8	52.6	54.5	56.4	63.8
Wyoming.............	49.1	50.3	51.6	52.8	54.1	59.0

SOURCE: Based on the relation of the United States Democratic percentages for 1920–4 and 1936 to the corresponding percentages for each of the states (representing the period 1916–44).

TABLE 9: Vote for Members of House of Representatives, 1928–1946

| | NUMBER OF VOTES (THOUSANDS) | | | | PERCENTAGE | | |
YEAR	U.S. TOTAL	DEMO-CRATIC	REPUBLI-CAN	OTHER	DEMO-CRATIC	REPUBLI-CAN	OTHER
1928	34,154	14,361	19,163	631	42.0	56.1	1.8
1930	24,777	11,044	13,032	700	44.6	52.6	2.8
1932	37,657	20,540	15,575	1,542	54.5	41.4	4.1
1934	32,530	17,385	13,558	1,588	53.4	41.7	4.9
1936	42,886	23,944	17,003	1,939	55.8	39.6	4.5
1938	36,236	17,611	17,047	1,577	48.6	47.0	4.4
1940	46,951	24,092	21,393	1,466	51.3	45.6	3.1
1942	28,074	12,934	14,203	937	46.1	50.6	3.3
1944	45,103	22,808	21,303	992	50.6	47.2	2.2
1946	34,410	15,212	18,422	776	44.2	53.5	2.3

SOURCE: 1928 through 1944 from Bureau of the Census; 1946, *Statistics of the Congressional Election of November 5, 1946,* issued by the Clerk of the House of Representatives.

The number of Congressmen elected by the two major and other parties in the 1928–46 and earlier elections is given in Table 10. It also shows the number of vacancies that occurred between the elections in November and the seating of the Congresses in the following March or January.

NUMBER OF CONGRESSMEN ELECTED

CONGRESS		REPUBLICANS	DEMOCRATS	OTHER
78th	1943–5	209	222	4
79th	1945–7	190	243	2
80th	1947–9	246	188	1

TABLE 10: Party Divisions of Senate and House of Representatives from 1855 (34th Congress) to 1947–9 (80th Congress)

CONGRESS	SENATE					HOUSE OF REPRESENTATIVES				
	NUMBER OF SENATORS	REPUBLICANS	DEMOCRATS	OTHER PARTIES	VACANT	NUMBER OF REPRESENTATIVES	REPUBLICANS	DEMOCRATS	OTHER PARTIES	VACANT
34th...1855–7	62	15	42	5	.....	234	108	83	43	.....
35th...1857–9	64	20	39	5	.....	237	92	131	14	.....
36th...1859–61	66	26	38	2	.....	237	113	101	23	.....
37th...1861–3	50	31	11	7	1	178	106	42	28	2
38th...1863–5	51	39	12	....	.....	183	103	80	....	.....
39th...1865–7	52	42	10	....	.....	191	145	46	....	.....
40th...1867–9	53	42	11	....	.....	193	143	49	....	1
41st...1869–71	74	61	11	....	2	243	170	73	....	.....
42d...1871–3	74	57	17	....	.....	243	139	104	....	.....
43d...1873–5	74	54	19	....	1	293	203	88	....	2
44th...1875–7	76	46	29	....	1	293	107	181	3	2
45th...1877–9	76	39	36	1	.....	293	137	156	....	.....
46th...1879–81	76	33	43	....	.....	293	128	150	14	1
47th...1881–3	76	37	37	2	.....	293	152	130	11	.....
48th...1883–5	76	40	36	....	.....	325	119	200	6	.....
49th...1885–7	76	41	34	....	1	325	140	182	2	1
50th...1887–9	76	39	37	....	.....	325	151	170	4	.....
51st...1889–91	84	47	37	....	.....	330	173	156	1	.....
52d...1891–3	88	47	39	2	.....	333	88	231	14	.....
53d...1893–5	88	38	44	3	3	357	126	220	8	.....
54th...1895–7	88	44	39	5	.....	357	246	104	7	.....
55th...1897–9	90	46	34	10	.....	357	206	134	16	1
56th...1899–1901	90	53	26	11	.....	357	185	163	9	.....
57th...1901–3	90	56	29	3	2	357	198	153	5	1
58th...1903–5	90	58	32	....	.....	386	207	178	....	1
59th...1905–7	90	58	32	....	.....	386	250	136	....	.....
60th...1907–9	92	61	29	....	2	386	222	164	....	.....
61st...1909–11	92	59	32	....	1	391	219	172	....	.....
62d...1911–13	92	49	42	....	1	391	162	228	1	.....
63d...1913–15	96	44	51	1	.....	435	127	290	18	.....
64th...1915–17	96	39	56	1	.....	435	193	231	8	3
65th...1917–19	96	42	53	1	.....	435	216	210	9	.....
66th...1919–21	96	48	47	1	.....	435	237	191	7	.....
67th...1921–3	96	59	37	....	.....	435	300	132	1	2
68th...1923–5	96	51	43	2	.....	435	225	207	3	.....
69th...1925–7	96	54	40	1	1	435	247	183	5	.....
70th...1927–9	96	48	47	1	.....	435	237	195	3	.....
71st...1929–31	96	56	39	1	.....	435	267	163	1	4
72d...1931–3	96	48	47	1	.....	435	220	[1]214	1	.....
73d...1933–5	96	36	59	1	.....	435	117	313	5	.....
74th...1935–7	96	25	69	2	.....	435	103	322	10	.....
75th...1937–9	96	17	75	4	.....	435	89	333	13	.....
76th...1939–41	96	23	69	4	.....	435	169	262	4	.....
77th...1941–3	96	28	66	2	.....	435	162	267	6	.....
78th...1943–5	96	37	58	1	.....	435	211	216	4	4
79th...1945–7	96	38	56	1	1	435	190	242	2	1
80th...1947–9	96	51	45	....	.....	435	245	188	1	1

[1] Democrats organized House, because of Republican deaths.

SOURCE: *Factual Campaign Information*, Office of the Secretary of the United States Senate, 1944 (revised).

TABLE 11: Party Membership in House of Representatives, 1854–1946

YEAR	DEMOCRATIC PER CENT OF TWO-PARTY MEMBERSHIP	PER CENT OF TOTAL MEMBERSHIP		
		DEMOCRATIC	REPUBLICAN	OTHER AND VACANCIES
1854	43.5	35.5	46.2	18.3
1856	58.7	55.3	38.8	5.9
1858	47.2	42.6	47.7	9.7
1860	28.4	23.6	59.6	16.8
1862	43.7	43.7	56.3	
1864	24.1	24.1	75.9	
1866	25.5	25.4	74.1	.5
1868	30.0	30.0	70.0	
1870	42.8	42.8	57.2	
1872	30.2	30.0	69.3	.7
1874	62.8	61.8	36.5	1.7
1876	53.2	53.2	46.8	
1878	54.0	51.2	43.7	5.1
1880	46.1	44.4	51.9	3.7
1882	62.7	61.5	36.6	1.9
1884	56.5	56.0	43.1	.9
1886	53.0	52.3	46.5	1.2
1888	47.4	47.3	52.4	.3
1890	72.4	69.4	26.4	4.2
1892	63.6	61.2	36.0	2.8
1894	29.7	29.2	68.5	2.3
1896	39.4	37.5	57.7	4.8
1898	46.8	45.6	51.8	2.6
1900	43.6	42.6	55.5	1.9
1902	46.2	46.1	53.6	.3
1904	35.2	35.2	64.8	
1906	42.5	42.5	57.5	
1908	44.0	44.0	56.0	
1910	58.5	58.3	41.4	.3
1912	69.5	66.7	29.2	4.9
1914	54.5	53.1	44.4	2.5
1916	49.3	48.3	49.7	2.0
1918	44.6	43.9	54.5	1.6
1920	30.6	30.3	69.0	.7
1922	47.9	47.6	51.7	.7
1924	42.6	42.1	56.8	1.1
1926	45.1	44.8	54.5	.7
1928	37.9	37.5	61.4	1.1
1930	49.3	49.2	50.6	.2
1932	72.8	71.9	26.9	1.2
1934	75.8	74.0	23.7	2.3
1936	78.9	76.5	20.5	3.0
1938	60.8	60.2	38.9	.9
1940	62.2	61.4	37.2	1.4
1942	50.6[1]	49.7	48.5	1.8
1944	56.0	55.6	43.7	.7
1946	43.4	43.2	56.3	.5

[1] Per cent elected, 51.5.

TABLE 12: Political Tides: Membership in Congress and Two-Party Vote for President, 1852–1946

YEAR	DEMOCRATIC PER CENT OF TWO-PARTY POPULAR VOTE FOR PRESIDENT	DEMOCRATIC PER CENT OF TWO-PARTY MEMBERSHIP		YEAR	DEMOCRATIC PER CENT OF TWO-PARTY POPULAR VOTE FOR PRESIDENT	DEMOCRATIC PER CENT OF TWO-PARTY MEMBERSHIP	
		HOUSE	SENATE			HOUSE	SENATE
1852	53.7			1900	46.8	43.6	34.1
1854		43.5	73.7	1902		46.2	35.6
1856	57.6	58.7	66.1	1904	40.0	35.2	35.6
1858		47.2	59.4	1906		42.5	32.2
1860	42.4	28.4	26.2	1908	45.5	44.0	35.2
1862		43.7	23.5	1910		58.5	46.2
1864	44.9	24.1	19.4	1912	64.4	69.5	53.7
1866		25.5	20.8	1914		54.5	58.9
1868	47.2	30.0	15.3	1916	51.7	49.3	55.8
1870		42.8	23.0	1918		44.6	49.5
1872	44.1	30.2	26.0	1920	36.1	30.6	38.5
1874		62.8	38.7	1922		47.9	45.7
1876	51.5	53.2	48.0	1924	34.8	42.6	42.6
1878		54.0	56.6	1926		45.1	49.5
1880	49.9	46.1	50.0	1928	41.2	37.9	41.1
1882		62.7	47.4	1930		49.3	49.5
1884	50.3	56.5	45.2	1932	59.1	72.8	62.1
1886		53.0	48.7	1934		75.8	73.4
1888	49.9	47.4	44.0	1936	62.2	78.9	81.3
1890		72.4	45.3	1938		60.8	75.0
1892	51.8	63.6	53.7	1940	55.0	62.2	70.2
1894		29.7	47.0	1942		50.6	60.0
1896	47.1	39.4	42.5	1944	53.8	56.0	57.8
1898		46.8	32.9	1946		43.4	46.9

TABLE 13: Indexes of Voting Flexibility, 1896–1936 (by rank of states in 1896–1904 index)

	1896–1904	1904–16	1916–24	1924–36
Idaho	6.34	2.27	1.74	1.47
Utah	6.00	2.21	1.41	1.24
Montana	5.55	1.97	1.83	1.57
Colorado	5.29	1.68	1.89	1.21
Nevada	5.14	1.75	1.54	1.60
Washington	4.31	2.45	1.85	1.77
Oregon	3.45	2.26	1.06	1.26
Nebraska	3.39	2.73	1.25	.86
South Dakota	3.37	2.07	1.59	1.28
Average	4.76	2.15	1.57	1.36
Kansas	3.00	2.03	1.29	.94
North Dakota	2.73	2.26	1.99	1.65
Minnesota	2.66	2.34	1.94	1.73
Wyoming	2.42	2.18	1.88	1.40
Michigan	2.13	1.55	1.50	1.36
Arkansas	2.05	.99	.26	.65
California	1.70	1.68	1.87	1.86
Ohio	1.54	1.50	1.38	1.08
Illinois	1.48	1.11	.98	1.08
Iowa	1.48	1.04	1.29	1.19
Wisconsin	1.08	1.26	1.69	1.75
Pennsylvania	1.02	1.10	1.03	1.19
Average	1.94	1.59	1.43	1.32
Missouri	.95	.39	.33	.53
Indiana	.94	.54	.38	.56
West Virginia	.58	.55	.21	.52
Maine	.08	1.50	1.19	.62
Mississippi	− .01	.19	.19	.24
Kentucky	− .11	.18	.28	.39
Delaware	− .18	.32	.56	.62
New Jersey	− .25	.39	.75	1.02
Tennessee	− .33	.17	.16	.50
Florida	− .34	.04	.60	.60
Vermont	− .35	1.40	.95	.87
New York	− .43	.19	.75	.94
Average	− .05	.49	.53	.62
Georgia	− .55	1.34	.29	.41
Connecticut	− .67	.74	.94	.88
Alabama	− .76	.23	.36	.57
North Carolina	− .80	−.14	−.04	.45
South Carolina	− .80	.11	.00	.06
Maryland	− .86	.34	.56	.67
Virginia	−1.08	.44	.21	.25
Rhode Island	−1.18	.84	.46	.53
Massachusetts	−1.31	.80	1.06	.83
Louisiana	−1.47	−.22	.46	.39
New Hampshire	−1.49	.97	.70	.47
Texas	−2.14	.45	.17	.43
Arizona	...	...	1.06	1.08
New Mexico	...	...	.36	.62
Oklahoma	...	...	.10	.58
Average	−1.09	.49	.45	.55

NOTE: Change in U.S. Democratic percentage of total vote for each period equals index of 1.00.

TABLE 14: Index of Business Activity, June and October 1854–1947 (per cent deviations from normal)

YEAR	JUNE	OCTOBER	YEAR	JUNE	OCTOBER
1854	+10	− 2	1901	+ 4	+ 4
1855	+ 4	+ 5	1902	+ 3	+ 3
1856	+10	+ 8	1903	+ 5	− 4
1857	+ 2	−10	1904	− 7	− 5
1858	− 9	− 6	1905	+ 9	+ 9
1859	+ 1	− 1	1906	+ 9	+11
1860	+ 2	+ 3	1907	+11	+ 8
1861	−10	− 8	1908	−17	−10
1862	− 1	0	1909	− 1	+ 9
1863	+ 2	+ 4	1910	+ 2	− 3
1864	+ 6	+ 3	1911	− 7	− 5
1865	−10	−13	1912	+ 3	+ 8
1866	+ 7	+10	1913	+ 6	+ 4
1867	0	0	1914	− 3	−10
1868	0	+ 2	1915	− 1	+ 7
1869	+ 5	+ 1	1916	+14	+16
1870	+ 4	− 5	1917	+13	+11
1871	+ 6	+ 6	1918	+ 7	+ 9
1872	+ 9	+12	1919	0	+ 2
1873	+ 8	+ 1	1920	+ 6	− 4
1874	− 3	− 6	1921	−26	−20
1875	− 8	−12	1922	− 6	+ 2
1876	−10	−11	1923	+15	+ 8
1877	−10	−10	1924	− 9	0
1878	− 8	− 8	1925	+ 5	+ 6
1879	− 7	+ 6	1926	+ 7	+10
1880	+ 6	+ 6	1927	+ 6	− 1
1881	+10	+ 9	1928	+ 3	+ 9
1882	+ 5	+ 8	1929	+16	+12
1883	+ 3	+ 2	1930	− 9	−21
1884	− 3	−10	1931	−25	−35
1885	−10	−10	1932	−48	−41
1886	+ 3	+ 3	1933	−20	−31
1887	+ 4	+ 7	1934	−27	−37
1888	− 1	+ 6	1935	−27	−19
1889	0	+ 6	1936	−11	− 7
1890	+11	+12	1937	− 2	−15
1891	+ 5	+13	1938	−36	−21
1892	+ 6	+ 5	1939	−18	+ 1
1893	+ 4	−19	1940	+ 1	+10
1894	−20	− 5	1941	+30	+32
1895	− 5	+ 6	1942	+29	+35
1896	− 7	−17	1943	+35	+41
1897	−10	− 1	1944	+34	+32
1898	+ 1	− 1	1945	+29	+ 6
1899	+ 4	+ 9	1946	+15	+23
1900	+ 7	− 5	1947	+24	

SOURCE: Cleveland Trust Company, Cleveland, Ohio.

TABLE 15: Illustration of Religion as a Factor in Presidential Elections: 1928, by States

STATE	CATHOLIC CHURCH MEMBERSHIP [1] (PER CENT)	DEPARTURE FROM NORMAL VOTING [2]
Alabama	3	−23
Arizona	63	−10
Arkansas	4	−11
California	47	+ 8
Colorado	36	0
Connecticut	58	+10
Delaware	34	− 4
Florida	7	−27
Georgia	1	−17
Idaho	14	0
Illinois	40	+ 7
Indiana	23	− 8
Iowa	26	+ 5
Kansas	23	− 8
Kentucky	17	−11
Louisiana	57	− 6
Maine	60	+ 3
Maryland	31	− 8
Massachusetts	65	+15
Michigan	47	+ 4
Minnesota	39	+16
Mississippi	4	−12
Missouri	34	− 7
Montana	49	+ 2
Nebraska	28	−10
Nevada	40	+ 1
New Hampshire	66	0
New Jersey	53	+10
New Mexico	81	−10
New York	46	+ 9
North Carolina	4	−17
North Dakota	34	+17
Ohio	34	0
Oklahoma	8	−23
Oregon	24	− 5
Pennsylvania	41	+ 5
Rhode Island	72	+ 8
South Carolina	1	− 3
South Dakota	33	+ 6
Tennessee	25	−12
Texas	24	−33
Utah	4	+ 3
Vermont	55	+10
Virginia	3	−20
Washington	32	+ 3
West Virginia	13	− 9
Wisconsin	45	+23
Wyoming	30	+ 5

[1] Bureau of the Census, 1926, Catholic Church membership as per cent of membership in all denominations.
[2] Normal two-party Democratic percentages based on 1924–32 experience (*Ballot Behavior*, pp. 35, 72–6) subtracted from actual two-party percentages in 1928.

TABLE 16: Illustration of Nationality as a Factor in Presidential Elections: 1940 ,1944, by States

STATE	POPULATION [1]		DEPARTURES FROM NORMAL VOTING [2]	
	Per Cent German	Per Cent Italian	1940	1944
Alabama..............	.38	.25	+ 2.9	− .4
Arizona..............	1.82	.48	− 1.1	− 4.9
Arkansas.............	.90	.16	+ 1.7	− 6.5
California............	5.46	4.17	+ 3.4	+ 3.7
Colorado.............	4.86	3.03	− 5.7	− 6.5
Connecticut..........	4.75	14.14	+ 2.6	+ 2.6
Delaware.............	2.33	4.31	+ 2.6	+ 3.0
Florida..............	1.53	.91	+ .4	− 3.0
Georgia..............	.28	.06	+ 7.5	− 1.2
Idaho...............	3.93	.62	− 1.5	− 2.9
Illinois..............	10.41	3.56	+ 2.0	+ 2.3
Indiana..............	5.70	.51	− 4.1	− 5.6
Iowa................	11.64	.39	+ .3	+ 1.4
Kansas..............	5.70	.31	− 5.1	− 7.5
Kentucky............	2.24	.17	+ .8	− 1.7
Louisiana............	1.27	2.30	+ .9	− 3.7
Maine...............	.36	.81	+10.3	+ 9.6
Maryland............	5.82	1.74	+ .8	− 5.5
Massachusetts........	1.65	7.59	+ 5.4	+ 5.9
Michigan............	7.54	2.02	+ 1.4	+ 3.6
Minnesota...........	12.78	.67	− 1.3	+ 1.2
Mississippi..........	.24	.25	+ 3.4	+ 3.3
Missouri............	7.24	1.08	− 4.6	− 4.9
Montana.............	5.65	1.18	− 1.8	− 5.1
Nebraska............	12.22	.65	− 9.6	−10.0
Nevada..............	4.23	5.90	− 2.8	− 7.1
New Hampshire.......	.95	1.03	+ 5.6	+ 5.0
New Jersey...........	8.54	12.55	− .1	− .1
New Mexico..........	1.17	.80	− 1.6	− 4.1
New York............	8.20	12.33	+ .5	+ 2.5
North Carolina........	.13	.04	+ 4.6	− 2.1
North Dakota........	8.01	.04	−12.3	− 7.0
Ohio................	7.66	2.71	− 1.5	− 3.1
Oklahoma............	1.59	.14	− 4.8	− 6.2
Oregon..............	5.93	1.03	− 5.1	− 5.4
Pennsylvania.........	5.06	6.37	+ 3.9	+ 3.0
Rhode Island.........	1.47	13.39	+ 5.7	+ 8.4
South Carolina........	.25	.04	− 1.0	− 3.2
South Dakota.........	10.73	.12	− 4.5	− 4.2
Tennessee............	.42	.22	+ 1.3	− 3.0
Texas...............	2.63	.37	− 3.0	− 2.8
Utah................	2.43	1.37	+ 1.9	+ .2
Vermont.............	.64	2.10	+ 7.9	+ 6.6
Virginia.............	.54	.32	− .3	− 5.8
Washington..........	5.57	1.43	+ 2.7	+ 3.0
West Virginia........	1.15	1.86	+ .5	− 1.1
Wisconsin...........	20.69	1.09	− 2.7	− 3.5
Wyoming............	4.08	1.66	+ .2	− 2.8

[1] Bureau of the Census, 1930, Population of German and Italian origin or parentage as per cent of total population.
[2] Normal two-party Democratic percentages in table 8 (U.S. 55 per cent for 1940 and 54 per cent for 1944) subtracted from the actual 1940 and 1944 two-party percentages in table 6.

References:

The Presidential Vote, 1896–1932, E. E. Robinson, Stanford University Press, 1934

They Voted for Roosevelt, E. E. Robinson, Stanford University Press, 1947

The Gallup Political Almanac for 1946, American Institute of Public Opinion, Princeton, 1946

The World Almanac (1948 and earlier editions), New York World-Telegram, 1948

Vote Cast in Presidential and Congressional Elections, 1928–1944 (Elections: 1944, No. 5, 1946), Bureau of the Census, U.S. Department of Commerce

Statistics of the Congressional Election of November 5, 1946, issued by the Clerk of the House of Representatives, 1947

A NOTE ON THE TYPE IN WHICH THIS BOOK IS SET

The text of this book is set in Caledonia, a Linotype face designed by W. A. Dwiggins. This type belongs to the family of printing types called "modern face" by printers —a term used to mark the change in style of type-letters that occurred about 1800. Caledonia borders on the general design of Scotch Modern, but is more freely drawn than that letter.

The book was composed, printed, and bound by Kingsport Press, Inc., Kingsport, Tennessee.

Correction - Title Page, 167, line 1

"1899" should be "1889"